Twayne's United States Authors Series

Sylvia E. Bowman, *Editor*

INDIANA UNIVERSITY

Harriet Beecher Stowe

HARRIET BEECHER STOWE

by JOHN R. ADAMS
San Diego State College

TWAYNE PUBLISHERS
A DIVISION OF G. K. HALL & CO., BOSTON

Library of Congress Catalog Card Number: 63-17370

ISBN 0–8057–0700–X

MANUFACTURED IN THE UNITED STATES OF AMERICA

To My Mother

Contents

Preface

HARRIET BEECHER STOWE has made three claims upon public attention: as woman, as legend, and as writer. The most significant of these, as well as the most neglected for many years, is that of the writer. Without her literary career Mrs. Stowe would have been a nonentity, and the legends are mere distortions of what and why she wrote.

Mrs. Stowe's writings are the subject of my book. Though a story worth telling may lose nothing by repetition, my purpose has been distinctly different from that of her biographers. When referring to her personality I have tried, as faithfully as possible, to show it in relation to her writings in order to explain them, rather than to follow the custom of biographers who have been more interested in what she did than in what she wrote.

The legendary Mrs. Stowe is undoubtedly the most enticing. The melodramatic play based upon *Uncle Tom's Cabin*, an adaptation with which she had no more connection than if it had been a Hollywood movie or a Broadway musical show, misrepresented the original novel to such a degree that it still controls some people's reactions to the author. She takes on the image of a fire-eating agitator, angelic or diabolical, and of a tireless worker on the underground railway. Later, as legend has it, she becomes the friend and advisor of Abraham Lincoln and inspires the emancipation of the slaves.

In another legend the girl Harriet assumes the form of an ugly duckling in the midst of imitation swans and genuine geese, her unappreciative relatives: the hell-fire-spouting father, holding forth on Sundays at Brimstone Corner; the blighted elder sister "schoolmarm"; the windbag younger brother, later the principal target in a monumental petty scandal; the henpecked husband; and an accompanying chorus of assorted Beechers and, as the years roll by, younger generations of assorted Stowes.

These are unjust exaggerations, although a natural response to the bland self-satisfaction of the family chronicles. The father was a genuinely eminent leader, an extraordinarily vigorous intellect. Sister Catherine became one of the greatest figures in the development of higher education for women and in the establishment of professional home economics. At the peak of his power Henry Ward Beecher was a spokesman as representative of his time as Dr. Harry Emerson Fosdick or Dr. Norman Vincent Peale are of theirs, although immeasurably more dynamic and influential.[1]

Calvin Stowe, in particular, was a scholar of high repute, a public speaker of no mean ability, a loyal helpmate and, above all, the stimulator of his wife's literary talents. While she was still an amateurish novice he wrote, "My dear, you must be a literary woman." This was not all: "God has written it in His book that you must be a literary woman, and who are we that we should contend against God?" Firmer support can hardly be asked. Her own comments on her early endeavors were on a lower level: "If I choose to be a literary lady, I have, I think, as good a chance of making profit by it as any one I know of." It was the husband who urged: "You must therefore make all your calculations to spend the rest of your life with your pen." Calvin Stowe not only encouraged his wife to write; his recollections gave her, years later, the best material for her best stories about the New England of his boyhood.[2]

The Lincoln legend, like the others, has an exceedingly slight basis in fact. Mrs. Stowe saw Lincoln once, in 1862, when she went to Washington to interview him privately for a magazine article and to ask a favor on behalf of her wounded son. As he met her he greeted her, according to her account, which is the only authority, as "the little lady who wrote the book that made this big war!" or in words to that effect, since the phraseology of the remark varies in different versions. But what does this prove? That President Lincoln was Chivalrous Abe as well as Honest, and—which is a truly remarkable tribute—that he could recall a novel published ten years previously (no evidence has been found that he had read it) and that he correctly associated the book with the author's name. When Nathaniel Hawthorne returned from his only meeting with Lincoln, he was convinced that the President had not the slightest idea of his identity, or of *The Scarlet Letter*, *The House of the Seven Gables*, or any of Hawthorne's other not inconsequential writings.³ The Lincoln legend shows that Mrs. Stowe was a famous public figure. It hardly indicates that she did in fact cause the Civil War or that Abraham Lincoln thought she did or thought that *she* would have thought she did.⁴

In her time Mrs. Stowe was eminent both at home and abroad. Her international reputation was of course based on *Uncle Tom's Cabin* (1852), her first novel. With such diverse personalities as Leo Tolstoi, Thomas Babington Macaulay, George Sand, and Heinrich Heine writing in eulogy, her eminence is undeniable. Tolstoi greeted the book as a great humanitarian document like *Les Misérables* and *A Tale of Two Cities*; and Heine, in stronger terms, associated it with the Bible. Macaulay praised it as "the most valuable addition that America has made to English literature"; but George Sand, like Tolstoi and Heine, stressed its moral rather than its literary greatness: "the genius of goodness, not that of the man of letters, but of the saint." Emerson's entry in his journal was true of readers abroad as well as at home: the lady, the cook, the chambermaid were equally enthralled. Like intellectuals and plain citizens everywhere, statesmen and monarchs were also enthralled by *Uncle Tom's Cabin*.⁵ Although not one of Mrs. Stowe's later books became an international best-seller, her reputation as a great American humanitarian endured.

To a generation persuaded that the greatest of American women writers is Emily Dickinson, it is probably impossible to explain why Mrs. Stowe not only held that position in the nineteenth century, but how she was also regarded as the greatest benefactor. Her prestige abroad was equal to that of Willa Cather or Pearl Buck, plus that of Jane Addams or Eleanor Roosevelt. Purely as a writer, she was admired by George Eliot, who reviewed *Dred* (1856) with enthusiasm, crediting it with "the enchantment of genius." The great Gladstone, during one of his periods as prime minister, praised *The Minister's Wooing* (1859) without reservation. Elizabeth Barrett Browning, whose literary standards were possibly more rigorous, declared of Mrs. Stowe that "she above all women (yes, and men of the age) has moved the world—and *for good*."⁶

At home Mrs. Stowe also fared well. When the great New England magazine, the *Atlantic Monthly*, was founded in 1857 she was one of the indispensable original contributors. Other magazine editors requested more writing from her than she could find time for, and the sales of her later books were gratifying. Such literary leaders as Longfellow, Lowell, and Whittier were charmed by her New England stories; and younger writers like Sarah Orne Jewett were proud to follow in her footsteps. The English novelist Charles Reade was led, through a fortunate misunderstanding, into new paths of documented reform fiction; and George Eliot was stimulated to write *Daniel Deronda* (1876), a study of racial tensions, by her recollections of *Dred*. Even Mark Twain, the Stowes' neighbor in Hartford, Connecticut, during her later years, held Mrs. Stowe in great respect. He is thought to have found help in her stories for *The Prince and the Pauper* (1882) and for the Nigger Jim episodes in *Huckleberry Finn* (1884).[7]

As professional literary historians know, neither the power nor the original charm of Mrs. Stowe's books has entirely vanished. The standard brief surveys, ranging from tolerant to commendatory, describe her best known fiction with the perspective and the caution due her reputation. In contrast, it is enlightening to note the more outspoken surprise of other readers, supposedly sophisticated, at their unexpected discoveries when they happen upon her books completely by chance. They respond to *Oldtown Folks* with an appreciative essay on "An Almost Lost American Classic," and they compare *The Minister's Wooing*, not too unfavorably, with Santayana's *The Last Puritan*. *Uncle Tom's Cabin*, they write, is more than a historical monument. They may decide that it is sociologically horrible or morally admirable, transparently Freudian or fascinatingly mythic; but it is neither dead nor dull. Almost inevitably, a serious adult reader will come from these books preaching—an effect which the author would have approved.[8]

Most of Mrs. Stowe's books (except *Uncle Tom's Cabin*) have been out of print, although not off library shelves, for a half century or more. Sufficient reasons for this neglect exist. To speak gently of them, they are not obviously or immediately exciting, and even conscientious scholars can be pardoned for reading only a few of the more than forty titles listed in the standard bibliographies. Yet the sampling method inevitably gives a false emphasis, for descriptions and appraisals reasonably accurate in themselves produce false impressions in the absence of essential background.

Consequently the legends about Mrs. Stowe which began in ignorance or prejudice have been nourished by this selectiveness. *Uncle Tom's Cabin* was a desperately controversial book when it was published. Its author, neither saint nor devil, was before everything else a writer; and the purpose of my book is to describe the kind of writer she was, not only in *Uncle Tom's Cabin* but in her later, more representative and characteristic books. To appreciate what kind of writer Mrs. Stowe was, I have used the simple method of reading and reflecting on everything I could find that she wrote, including journalistic scraps inconsequential in themselves. More than two hundred uncollected articles and stories from magazines and newspapers are more than a bulky addition to her collected writings; they also help toward understanding how she worked and to what purpose. I am not sure that any other reader has subjected himself to this discipline (or should), but experience has persuaded me that acquaintance with the whole work is necessary for the proper appreciation of its parts.[9] A century of commentary is not to be disregarded, but much of it was irrelevant in its day and is completely beside the point now.

In a resolute effort to avoid myth-making, I have treated my material conservatively rather than imaginatively. To resurrect literary corpses only to demonstrate that they unquestionably are corpses is unproductive as well as unkind, and I agree that Mrs. Stowe's career has implications beyond any that I have suggested. Mrs. Stowe was not only the most famous American female writer of her time—the one woman whom Hawthorne could not have justly included in his 1855 denunciation of the "d——d mob of scribbling women"; she persists as either a symbol or a symptom of American culture. Perhaps this is because some of the conflicts that shaped her, the principles and prejudices that she accepted, are basic and enduring—even in a new age of great change and social reorganization. My readers, I am confident, will answer such implicit questions with assurance.

JOHN R. ADAMS

Chronology

1811 June 14, birth of Harriet Elizabeth Beecher, daughter of Lyman and Roxana Beecher, at Litchfield, Connecticut.

1816 Death of Roxana Beecher.

1824 Harriet's earliest preserved school composition, "Can the Immortality of the Soul be Proved by the Light of Nature?" Removal to Hartford, attends and teaches school at the Hartford Female Seminary, run by her elder sister.

1825 Composition of a tragedy in blank verse, "Cleon" (unfinished).

1832 Removal of the Beecher family to Cincinnati, Ohio.

1833 Harriet's first writings published in *Western Monthly Magazine*.

1836 January 6, marriage to Calvin Stowe (born 1802); September 29, birth of first children, twin girls. Anti-abolitionist riots in Cincinnati.

1849 Cholera epidemic in Cincinnati causes the death of the Stowes' infant son.

1850 Return to New England when Calvin Stowe receives an appointment to the faculty of Bowdoin College at Brunswick, Maine. July 8, birth of Charles Edward, the last of Harriet and Calvin Stowe's seven children.

1851 June 5, first installment of *Uncle Tom's Cabin* in the *National Era*, followed by book publication in 1852.

1852 Removal to Andover, Massachusetts, when Calvin Stowe joins the faculty of Andover Theological Seminary.

1853 First of three visits to Europe (others in 1856 and in 1859), as described in *Sunny Memories of Foreign Lands* (1854).

1856 Publication of *Dred*, Mrs. Stowe's second novel.

1857 Death by drowning of her eldest son, Henry. First contribution to the *Atlantic Monthly* (Vol. I, no. 1).

1859   Publication of *The Minister's Wooing,* Mrs. Stowe's first completed New England novel, after serialization in the *Atlantic Monthly.*

1862   Publication of *The Pearl of Orr's Island,* after serialization in the *Independent.*

1863   Death of Lyman Beecher.

1864   Removal to Hartford, Connecticut, after Calvin Stowe's retirement from teaching.

1869   Publication in the *Atlantic Monthly* of Mrs. Stowe's sensational article on Lord Byron's incest, followed by an expanded version in book form, *Lady Byron Vindicated* (1870). Publication of *Oldtown Folks,* her most substantial novel of New England, without prior magazine publication.

1873   Publication of *Palmetto-Leaves,* descriptive sketches in praise of Florida, her winter residence from 1868 to 1884.

1878   Publication of *Poganuc People,* her last novel, after being serialized in the *Christian Union.*

1886   August 6, death of Calvin Stowe, at Hartford, Connecticut.

1889   First official biography of Harriet Beecher Stowe, by Charles Edward Stowe, her son; and first unofficial biography, by Florine Thayer McCray.

1896   July 1, death of Harriet Beecher Stowe. Publication of *Writings,* in sixteen volumes, followed by an official biography (1898) by Annie Fields, a friend of many years.

Harriet Beecher Stowe

CHAPTER 1

Early Years

THE ESSENCE of Harriet Beecher's early life can be expressed in the word "subservience." Deprived of a mother's protection, the little girl was overwhelmed by her father's rugged character and doctrinal strictness. In late girlhood she was bound by an elder sister's equally stern discipline; and upon her marriage to Calvin Stowe she was besieged by poverty, poor health, and the demands of a rapidly increasing family. Thus did Harriet Beecher Stowe, both as maid and wife, learn through forty years the sufferings of those who are oppressed and subservient.

I *Harriet's Parents*

From the years of her earliest recollection Harriet found cause to brood over her position in the Beecher family. She was the youngest daughter and the seventh child of Roxana Foote Beecher, Lyman's first and favorite wife who, having given birth to nine of Lyman's children, contentedly died. Of the eight children who remained to mourn their mother, the eldest was Catherine and the two youngest, Henry Ward, two years Harriet's junior, and baby Charles.

Though dead and buried, Roxana was not forgotten. Her character, idyllic in its perfection, could not have wielded in life more influence over her children than it did in their memories. As family legend she gained power through Lyman's marriage, two years later, to Harriet Porter, a woman to be respected but hardly to be remembered as equal in human kindness to the lamented Roxana. Throughout Henry Ward's life and in spite of a literal impossibility, since at Roxana's death he was too young to have retained any recollections of her, Harriet's brother stoutly maintained that his mother had been the greatest influence upon him. Harriet held the same belief, though her own memories were but a scanty three, and two of them were of rebukes to the children for making too much noise and for eating tulip bulbs under the misapprehension that they were onions.[1]

The surviving parent, Lyman Beecher, was the type of man in whom energy is easily mistaken for genius. A thorough fundamentalist, the head of the family was a fiery evangelist for the Lord and the Beechers. In his family relationships Lyman was a bully of the worst stripe: a benevolently intentioned and systematically complete bully. It is difficult to know which alarmed his children more, his customary sternness or the moments of capricious high spirits which were vented upon rather than shared with them. If Lyman Beecher spared the rod, the reason was that he wielded more powerful instruments of torture, the most successful being dialectic and the threat of hell-fire which, as a disciple of Jonathan Edwards, he was adept at unleashing. In his logical battles with his children, which he considered admirable discipline for them, he loved to befuddle and humble them, never permitting them privileges because of their tender years. As a result, Henry Ward confessed that he had never felt at ease with his father; he had always been so conscious of the restrictive vigilance of the old Calvinist.[2]

In the Beecher family religious instruction was no weekly formality, for indoctrination was carried on continuously through daily family worship. Lyman knew exactly what he demanded of his children; he insisted that the boys become ministers and carry on his work, as eventually the seven who reached maturity did. The girls' future concerned him less, as there was little a girl need do in those days except marry, preferably a preacher. Consequently, or so Harriet was convinced, except for terrifying his daughters with the danger of hell, he neglected them, and much of her own girlhood was saddened by the slight esteem in which she seemed to be held. Lyman's proud declaration that she was a genius, a statement made when she was about seven years old, could have satisfied her only in part, for he immediately qualified it by the wish that she might have been a boy. As much feminine genius as was needed in the Beecher household was already manifest, in the father's view, in the oldest daughter Catherine, twelve years Harriet's senior.

Undoubtedly the lives of the Beecher children included happiness and jollity, as on the regular nutting excursions when their father romped like a boy and Harriet was allowed to dress and play like her brothers. In her later stories Mrs. Stowe often dwelt upon the advantages of a New England upbringing, but she did not even then forget the neglect she had suffered as a child and as a female. For her there were only fleeting escapes from the righteously harsh rule of a father who did not know his own blighting strength.[3]

II *Sister Catherine*

Nor was the second decade of her life to be happier than the first. A difficult enough period for young Christians of the Beecher tradition, the time of conversion was more than normally hard for Harriet, who at twelve years had been sent from the family home at Litchfield, her birthplace, to Hartford to be placed under the discipline and direction of her stern twenty-three-year-old sister. An orphanage would have been as home-like as the Hartford Female Seminary, for in Catherine the father's bullying instincts were reproduced and emphatically underscored.

For Catherine, poor soul, more than a word of extenuation is needed. Endowed with an intellect beyond most men's, she was less the victim of class or sex discrimination than of a vindictive fate. At a suitable age she had become happily engaged to a professor at Yale University who had died in a shipwreck before undergoing the ritual of a Presbyterian conversion. Although a man of high idealism and exemplary habits, Professor Fisher was considered in the Beecher household to be nonetheless irretrievably damned, unless he had squeezed into heaven by a last-minute declaration. Of this there were unfortunately no evidences, nor did the young man's character point in the direction of strict Calvinism.

From worry over her fiancé's soul and from natural grief that was not to be assuaged by his legacy of two thousand dollars, Catherine remained for years near mental collapse. In this melancholy state of mind she continued until she was saved by a grim determination, since personal happiness was denied her forever, to do good for others.

Catherine consecrated herself to the cause of female education. Using Professor Fisher's legacy as a nucleus, she gathered funds to establish the Hartford Female Seminary, and Harriet became one of her first victims. A gorgon in her later years, Catherine was in early womanhood already a formidable creature, unfitted by either temperament or training for the work she undertook. Self-admittedly she had been poorly educated at Miss Pierce's school, of which she spoke slightingly; and she was no doubt inexpert in some of the subjects she essayed: Latin, for which she coached two weeks, and moral philosophy, upon which she embarked equally unprepared. Her self-confidence was ample, for her rule was to regard herself as acting precisely as God, had He been a female educator, would have chosen to act. That viewpoint solved all her difficulties, she said, and dispelled all her doubts.[4]

Though Catherine must, in these early years, have taught superficially in her struggles with chemistry, rhetoric, logic, history, algebra, and natural philosophy, as well as Latin and moral philosophy, she was from the first a perfect disciplinarian. Harriet was twelve when she was delivered over to this stern guardian. When the child was discovered writing a poetic tragedy, Catherine bade her abandon such foolish vanity and set her to studying Bishop Butler's *The Analogy of Religion, Natural and Revealed, to the Course and Constitution of Nature.* As soon as Harriet was able to assist with the teaching, Catherine kept her so busy that the younger girl became dangerously nervous; she groaned and cried in her bed at night and laughed loudly and irrationally throughout the day. Her work was a burden to her; she felt that her life was wasted in caring for kindergarten "animals" (AF, pp. 49, 63).

III *Harriet's Conversion*

Simultaneously, during this decade of Harriet's teens, while the sister overbore, the distant father—who had left his pastorate at Litchfield in 1826 and had settled in Boston to do battle against the Unitarians and Harvard University—pursued her through the stages of her exhausting conversion to Christ.

The basic outlines of Lyman Beecher's Calvinism are shocking and frightening to the intellectually immature. For him, Jonathan Edwards (1703-58) was its chief exemplar and expositor. According to this greatest of divines—as his disciple interpreted him—Man was by nature actively evil, in spite of being endowed with will sufficient to withstand evil. Man was free to be good, certain to be wicked, and undoubtedly fit after this turbulent life only for those everlasting hell-fires which a just God had provided for his future abode. Escape? Through human effort there was none. Hope? One alone, the mercy of a pitying God for the favored among a sinful people. Assurance? None whatever. To feel one's soul safe was, to a man of Beecher's creed, a pitiful delusion. Whenever he discovered members of his flock flirting with the dangerous idea, he hurried to pay them pastoral visits to warn against this suggestion of the Devil.

As no one has pointed out more clearly than Mrs. Stowe in several of her novels, within this system compounded of sin and hell-fire which is too easily labeled Puritanism, multitudes of distinctions could be drawn. A rich dialectic exhilarated the theologians, providing exercises in logical agility that were the joy of acute minds such as Lyman Beecher's. For a child like Harriet in her teens, however, the harsh simplicity of the outline was all that was visible. She knew only that her salvation depended upon being scared out of her wits.

Later, when the diversion of traveling and the pleasure of young companions had restored apparent happiness so that she ceased to wish for an early death, she could still look back yearningly upon the memory of her mother. If Roxana had lived, Harriet believed, she might have spared her daughter much of the useless agony of salvation. Reading the Book of Job was not a comforting substitute. The display of God's power and strict justice appalled her, and her only consolation was her faith in the mercy and compassion of Jesus.[5]

That Jesus loved her, she at last became convinced, and in his companionship she found perfectly what her daily life supplied only imperfectly. Her work as teacher was one continued vexation to her, symbolizing the world from which she retreated to the arms of the Great Lover. Against all of her father's principles, she resolved never again to doubt her salvation as Jesus' lover; but she remained for many years weak in body and subject to periods of petulance and irritability. With every reason to feel the opposite, she set about trying consciously to develop a spirit of kindliness by remembering her happy hours and by allowing the others to slip from her memory.

IV Cincinnati and Marriage to Calvin Stowe

During eight years Harriet had been separated from the head of her family by her Hartford bondage. If there had been no relief in this separation from her father, neither was their reunion (1832), in the mass removal of the Beechers from Boston to Cincinnati, of immediate comfort. On the contrary, the change restored two masters over her, for she was to continue as assistant to Catherine in a new female college while living in the home and hence under the control of her father, now president of the eminent but insecure Lane Theological Seminary.

Cincinnati, the border settlement of mushroom growth that Lyman had glowingly described as the London of the West, appeared at first to the Connecticut-bred girl merely as an uncouth town. The father might excite himself with visions of saving the entire West for Jonathan Edwards, but the daughter was absorbed in the annoying, petty problems of running an elementary school. Her exhausted mind, she felt, was sinking to its death. Thought and emotion alike pained her, and she passed half her time busied with such trifles as quills or papers dropped on the floor.

In this crisis, meditating upon Mme. de Staël's *Corinne*, a popular romance which had found its way into the Beecher household, Harriet reflected almost philosophically upon the emotional starvation of America. Morbid and deep feelings, when repressed, she recognized, reduce a human soul to dust and ashes. Thought might have dawned seriously upon her had she not succeeded in arousing herself from melancholy reflection through the dual escape into what may be flatteringly called Literature and Love.

Thought, not being a marketable product, was held in abeyance. Instead, she composed a few magazine sketches and sentimental stories which, in addition to winning her a prize of fifty dollars, started her upon a long and eventually splendid literary career. Meanwhile, having hearkened to the call of Love, she was fully occupied with her growing family. If she had sought release from Beecherism in marrying Calvin Stowe, she was to be grievously disappointed; for Calvin, though he did not imperiously impose his will upon Harriet as her father had done, had his own effective way of regulating her conduct. The first children, twin girls born on September 29, 1836—the marriage had occurred on January 6 of the same year—were followed by five others. Within four years of the wedding ceremony four children had been born to them; and six of their seven offspring, the last born in 1850, survived childhood. Harriet was bound more closely to household tasks than ever before, and there is evidence to suggest that she was sometimes tempted to regret having married the good soul out of sympathy with him over the death of his first wife.

That pathetic fate, household martyrdom, was preparing for her; and except for her poverty she might have elevated herself to that station. Since there was money in the world, she resolved to help support the family—by writing. The Beechers had long complained about the poverty suffered by the Lord's servants. The children, Henry Ward in the van, grew tired of living from one Sunday collection to the next; and after Harriet's marriage the lack of money became the most intense goad to commercialization of her abilities. When she said in her later years that she wrote for money, the statement was as nearly true as its simplicity permitted.

The husband, although a charming and amusing man in hours of relaxation, was nearly ten years her senior and of a predominantly solemn cast of mind. In youth he had been a sober, earnest student; and his later experiences as teacher of Greek and theology at Dartmouth College and at Lane Seminary had made him mentally more nearly her father's contemporary than Harriet's. A sincere servant of the Lord, Calvin Stowe was President Lyman Beecher's first professorial convert to the idea of saving the West for orthodoxy. For his piety Harriet respected and honored him, as well as for his broad scholarship in philology, a subject unfortunately of no great interest to her. By far the strongest tie between them at the beginning was their common affection for his dead wife, Eliza, who had also been the daughter of a distinguished theologian—a love so enduring that throughout their lives Calvin and Harriet might have been seen hand in hand before Eliza's portrait upon every anniversary of her birthday, communing with her.[6]

From the first Harriet pitied this sad, learned man without becoming passionately excited by him. On the morning of her marriage she wrote in italics to a girlhood friend that she felt "*nothing at all*" (AF, 91). For years she was not enthusiastic about Calvin. After the birth of the third child she wrote an old friend that she could speak well of her marriage "after all" (AF, 97), and this admission was about as far as she would go. In 1841 she still felt herself destined to an early death and she wavered between devotion to her writing or to her children. In her weakened health—she was at one time near prostration from the death of her brother George—rainy days would reduce her to an extreme in which she became so sick of the smells of wet clothes, sour meat, sour milk "and sour everything" (AF, 110), that she felt she would never care to eat again. Only God sustained her, and He seemed far, far away: she was more likely to go to Him than to find Him coming to her.

It was the promise of a new day when Professor Stowe, deserting Lyman's Lane, received an appointment (1850) to the faculty of his alma mater, Bowdoin College at Brunswick, Maine.

V *Forty Years of Subservience*

And what, the reader may ask, through all these early years, may be said of Harriet herself? Except for her writing, the main story of her first forty years is the record of what she bore from others. This sad, repressed life was eventually, of course, not so unproductive as it seemed. Without her family's being exactly as it was, she could never have written her books exactly as she did. Catherine's life was essential for *The Minister's Wooing*, Calvin Stowe's for *Oldtown Folks*. The cholera epidemics of Cincinnati found their place in *Dred*. From her early sketch "Uncle Tim" in the *Western Monthly Magazine* to her book *Poganuc People* forty-odd years later, Lyman Beecher's character, life, and ancestry furnished details without which she could not have worked; and over this same period of time the dead mother, Roxana, and the dead infant son furnished equally essential dreams. For her material, Mrs. Stowe was more indebted to her family than most novelists have been.

On a less objective level these early repressions were no less significant; Mrs. Stowe's smouldering nature, when she ceased to be a wanderer in the strange country of the West, devised illusory compensations for the scanty freedom of her early years. Until 1850, however, she had attempted no estimate of herself as an individual. Life had been too hard for her, and she had taken refuge from it in the love of Jesus. To mistrust the world, to see it as the abode of cruelty and injustice, was a philosophy that she dared not confess to herself, though it was the one by which she lived.

Once the foreign environment of Cincinnati was thrown off, she began to feel better. Every stage of the journey that carried her towards New England lightened her burdens by taking her farther from at least two strong-willed members of her family, and one can see how, with the release of this pressure and the improvement in health which accompanied it, the frustrated woman might throw herself into a work of self-expression.[7] Professor Stowe's appointment to the faculty of Bowdoin College held a world of promise for his wife as well as for him. This promise, though genuine, was slow of fulfillment, and Mrs. Stowe's mind during the period immediately preceding and covering the writing of *Uncle Tom's Cabin* was still turbulent and restless.

When reading her letters from these early years, it is impossible to picture her as her early biographers suggest: a great soul impelled to expression by an unselfish love of humanity. In her own words she is revealed as an overworked housewife of forty, harassed by debt, relatives, personal sorrows, and family difficulties. Thus her *Uncle Tom's Cabin*, when it came, was her declaration of independence, her revolution, and her emancipation proclamation. Entirely aside from its qualities of melodrama or from its contribution to a complex social problem, the book had the force of a manifesto. With explosive power it shrieked against the indignity of subservience, and it offered the consolation of fellowship to frustrated humanity. It was an assertion of individual rights more easily understood in the 1850's than was Emerson's, Thoreau's, or Whitman's.

CHAPTER 2

Early Writings

M RS. STOWE'S APPRENTICESHIP was long. Within the framework of her modest ambitions it was rewarding. Negligible as her sketches and stories were, they earned her a minor place among the minor women writers for the minor magazines of the day. Some of them were reprinted in her first book, *The Mayflower* (1843), and others in an enlarged edition published after the success of *Uncle Tom's Cabin*. The majority were never collected. As a body, they clearly show the direction of her talents and the public for which she planned to write.

I   The Mayflower

The little volume called *The Mayflower* was as modest as its subtitle suggested: "Sketches of Scenes and Characters among the Descendants of the Puritans." The stories themselves, typical of the domestic fiction of the time, exhibited neither the strength nor the originality to suggest the later success and fame of their author. From the very first sketch the reader must resign himself to the familiar looseness in plot and characterization of the household fiction of the gift annuals and the ladies' magazines.

"Love *versus* Law," as this longish tale is called, is built in the casual way popular before Poe in *Tales of the Grotesque and Arabesque* (1840) and Hawthorne in *Twice-Told Tales* (1837) had introduced conscious unity of effect. Starting with some gentle reflections on Christian old age, "Love *versus* Law" progresses to a characterization of Deacon Enos Dudley, who is contrasted with his fellow officer, Deacon Abrams. When interest has been aroused in these two gentlemen, they are both dropped from the story—Deacon Abrams permanently

—while the action moves into the bosom of the Jones family. Two orphaned "girls," to use the author's word, the elder verging on forty and the younger just eighteen, introduce a new complication; for their dead father has cheated Deacon Enos out of five hundred dollars, and the only way in which he can collect is by taking the money from the legacy of the younger girl, the beautiful and tender Susan. Understandably enough, he hesitates.

Mrs. Stowe's story is not yet quite begun, for another family is needed to save Susan from unhappy poverty. Uncle Jaw Adams, a crabbed and contentious New Englander, has long been at odds with his neighbors, suing or threatening to sue them for innumerable grievances, fancied or real. At the moment, his heart is set on collecting damages from the Jones girls, because their father and he had never agreed on the exact boundaries between their farms. Solely for the reader's benefit, the whole story of the Jones-Adams feud is poured into good Deacon Enos' unwilling ears. When all the familiar details have tumbled out in a torrent of colloquialisms, the author pauses to announce: "But all this while the deacon had been in a profound meditation concerning the ways and means of putting a stop to a quarrel that had been his torment from time immemorial, and just at this moment a plan had struck his mind which our story will proceed to unfold."[1]

This promise of action is further delayed to introduce one other key character, the son of old Uncle Jaw. Young Joseph Adams has been away at college, and the Deacon's plan is the simple one of inducing the boy to marry Susan Jones, thus settling the feud between the families without recourse to the ugly "law" of the title. In the spirit of "love" he plans to contribute to the young folks his five-hundred-dollar claim against the Jones estate.

From this point the complications diminish, and the match between the young lovers proceeds without genuine obstacle. Of course the stern and inconsiderate older sister fails to realize the meaning of love to a delicate young girl; and of course the hardheaded father forbids his son to court the daughter of a traditional enemy. Against the basic goodness of human nature these demonstrations mean nothing. All such people are fundamentally good, Mrs. Stowe shows, once their better natures are appealed to, and love is bound to win. Thus this New England Romeo and Juliet, on a suitably modest scale, reach the happy ending of consummated love. The final paragraph of the tale is significant enough to quote:

> And, accordingly, many happy years flew over the heads of the young couple in the Stanton place, long after the hoary hairs of their kind benefactor, the deacon, were laid with reverence in the dust. Uncle Jaw was so far wrought upon by the magnanimity of the good old man as to be very materially changed for the better. Instead of quarreling in real earnest all around the neighborhood, he confined himself merely to battling the opposite side of every question with his son; which, as the latter was somewhat of a logician, afforded a pretty good field for the exercise of his powers; and he was heard to declare, at the funeral of the old deacon, that "after all, a man got as much, and maybe more, to go along as the deacon did, than to be all the time fisting and jawing;" "though I tell you what it is," said he, afterward, " 'taint every one that has the deacon's *faculty*, anyhow."[2]

The connections between this tale and Mrs. Stowe's life are obvious. Silence Jones is not exactly Catherine Beecher; yet her relationship with her younger sister is similar to Catherine's with Harriet. The contentious Uncle Jaw is not Lyman Beecher; but the relationship between him and his son is precisely that of the elder and younger Beechers. Young Joseph Adams is not Henry Ward Beecher; yet Susan's pride in him, especially as valedictorian, is precisely that which Harriet took in her favorite brother. "If ever a woman feels proud of her lover," she was to write in *Dred*, years later, "it is when she sees him as a successful speaker."[3]

In addition to such personal details, the story owed to Mrs. Stowe's past its whole New England setting. There are elements of realism here, local color, especially in touches of dialect. This last was no novelty in 1843, since well before this date two New England ladies had established themselves, through magazine sketches and complete novels, as local colorists of note. The names of Catharine M. Sedgwick and Lydia H. Sigourney, now almost forgotten, were among the brightest. The latter especially, who contributed to over three hundred different magazines, was both the Edna St. Vincent Millay and the Kathleen Norris of her age.

In Mrs. Sigourney's little-studied *Sketch of Connecticut, Forty Years Since,* published in 1824, a true forerunner of Mrs. Stowe's work is found. Although there is much of the literary lady about Mrs. Sigourney—with her elegant manners and her chapter headings from Goldsmith, Warton, and other proper poets—her book hits most of the topics Mrs. Stowe later developed. Like Mrs. Stowe, she enjoyed references to Saturday night baked beans and other such local customs; and, like her, she also breathed the full spirit of love for the land. Writing of Connecticut, Mrs. Sigourney said, precisely as Mrs. Stowe would have: "There, was exhibited the singular example of an aristocracy, less intent upon family aggrandizement, than upon becoming illustrious in virtue."[4]

Dialect abounds in the *Sketch of Connecticut,* but it is restricted, as in "Love *versus* Law," to the humble characters, and especially to a certain Farmer Larkin:

> Your ha-ath too, is as clean as a cheeny tea-cup, Ma'am. I hate to put my coarse huffs on it. But I ha'nt been used to seein' kiverlids spread on the floor to walk on. We are glad to get 'em to kiver us up with a nights. This looks like a boughten one . . . Tis exceedin' curous (110).

There is a full store of such talk, for Mrs. Sigourney's Farmer Larkin is as garrulous a man as Sam Lawson of Mrs. Stowe's later *Oldtown Folks* and *Sam Lawson's Oldtown Fireside Stories*:

> But Tim, the third child, he's the boy for larnin'. He took a prodigious likin' to books, when he was a baby; and if you only show'd him one, he's put it rite into his mouth, and stop squallin'. He 'ant but eleven year old now; and when he gets a newspaper, there's no *whoa* to him, no more than to our black ox when he sees the haystack, till he's read it clear through, advertisements and all (112).

This is truly the New England manner as Mrs. Stowe also understood it.

The Mayflower volume of 1843 contained fifteen sketches, several of which would repay as careful study as "Love *versus*

Law." In brief, *The Mayflower* foreshadows much of Mrs. Stowe's later writing. "Trials of a Housekeeper" was the first of many reactions to the servant problem. "Let Every Man Mind his own Business" was her first contribution to the temperance crusade for which, following her father's lead, she was always ready to say a kindly word. Her reforming zeal showed mildly for the cause of special Sunday services for children ("The Sabbath"), kinder treatment of tradespeople ("The Seamstress"), and greater financial support for religious institutions ("So Many Calls"). The first pathetic death scenes of her long series of them were to be found in "Uncle Tim" and in "Little Edward," in which the demise of a perfect child was recounted.

Aside from these themes that she was to develop later, the half-dozen New England sketches in the book, the only ones that justified the subtitle, thinly covered ground that she was subsequently to cultivate thoroughly. "Old Father Morris," the best designed of the series, presented an old-fashioned type of preacher. "Cousin William," planned along the same lines as "Love *versus* Law," introduced in Mrs. Abigail Evetts a busybody or reformer gone wrong. "The Sabbath" contained in its opening section a feeling description of church services in the old days.

"Uncle Tim," another in this New England series, was not only the most famous of the group—it was a prize winner—but was highly enough esteemed to be reprinted in 1834, soon after its appearance in James Hall's *Western Monthly Magazine*. A booklet of fifty-two pages, it appeared as *A New England Sketch*, with Mr. Gilman's publisher's notice on the reverse of the title page: "The following story was introduced to the public through the Western Monthly Magazine, a popular periodical; and the publisher's only object in throwing it before the community in this form, is that an effort so successful to delineate the character of New Englanders, by one of their daughters, may be preserved."[5]

"Throwing it before the community," an inept phrase with which to introduce a new writer's effort, is a marvel of elegant flattery in comparison with Catherine Beecher's well-meant but patronizing comments in her preface to *The Mayflower*. Without conscious malice, the elder sister was only following her bent, for she had admired Harriet's writing sufficiently to allow some of it to be published as her own. She would not try to praise her sister's sketches, Catherine said, describing them coldly as "written by a young mother and housekeeper in the first years of her novitiate." Her own interest as editor she confessed to be solely a general one in moral fiction as a type of writing preferable to the frivolous stories of Dickens; and she offered *The Mayflower* as an example of what might be attempted, without vouching for Harriet's "qualifications" for doing the work well. Aside from comments on the low moral tone and the disrespect for governesses shown by the regrettable Dickens, most of Catherine's preface was a sermon on purity. Directed to parents and clergymen, it concluded with the thought that whatever was good in Harriet's work could be traced to the excellent education Catherine had given her.

The Mayflower was no sensation. Harper and Brothers discontinued it within a few years, and it was forgotten until after the success of *Uncle Tom's Cabin*, when it was republished (except for a single sketch, "So Many Calls") as part of a much larger collection of articles and stories called *The May Flower, and Miscellaneous Writings* (1855). The twenty-one new sketches were in general similar to the original fifteen. Two more temperance tales appeared besides "Let Every Man Mind his own Business," strengthening Mrs. Stowe's position as a consistent prohibitionist rather than as one who merely favored prohibition. A few poems were also added, but the only contribution showing a new interest was "The Two Altars"—written in 1851—a strong attack on Negro slavery, a subject which had meant so little to Mrs. Stowe in 1843 that no allusion to it can be found in the entire *Mayflower*.

The commercial failure of her first collection of stories did not perturb Mrs. Stowe as much as might be expected, for she regarded book publication as a sideline. The compilation had in all probability been, as Catherine hinted in the preface, not Harriet's idea but Catherine's. Their joint textbook, a school geography published in 1833, had likewise been Catherine's plan, for she was the educator in the family and the senior collaborator on the book. Thus when *The Mayflower* led to no permanent alliance with the publishing firm of Harper and Brothers, Harriet shed no tears and uttered no lamentations.

In truth, at this time her ambitions were still held at the level of periodical publication. Books were a distant world beyond her reach, whereas magazines were as near as her fellow members of Cincinnati's literary Semi-Colon Club. She knew personally editors James Hall of the *Western Monthly Magazine* and E. D. Mansfield of the Cincinnati *Chronicle.* Other periodicals were almost as easily reached, and they paid two dollars a page for sketches that she could turn out between her housekeeping chores. In comparison with this assured income, small as it was, the financial returns from books were more than doubtful. Even *Uncle Tom's Cabin,* her first longer work, was originally written for a periodical. Intended as a few short sketches, it grew into two volumes, but subsequent book publication was looked upon merely as a problematical addition to the original three hundred dollars received from the *National Era.*

The effect of this attitude toward writing can be seen in her work from the beginning to the end of her career. Even in her later years, when her books sold well, they were first published in magazines—with only *Dred* and *Oldtown Folks* as significant exceptions. She wrote, that is, from month to month, or usually from week to week, under constant strain and without any chance to revise.

For an understanding of Mrs. Stowe's writings, early or late, a glance at the magazines which accepted her work is essential. The logical place to begin is the *Western Monthly Magazine* of Cincinnati, her first market.

II *Contributions to Cincinnati Publications*

When the Beechers reached Cincinnati in October, 1832, the city's literary colony was agog over the promised new magazine, the *Western Monthly Magazine,* to be started the following January. Actually, the *Western Monthly* was not entirely new, for it was a continuation of the *Illinois Monthly Magazine,* which had been issued since October, 1830. Nevertheless, the establishment of a high-class literary journal in Cincinnati was the cause of justifiable excitement.

No less enticing was the character of the editor, Judge James Hall, whom Harriet Beecher soon met. Hall had been soldier, lawyer, and politician, as well as jurist, writer, and editor. His manner was dynamic, and his literary work was dominated by consciously held theories, which he expressed repeatedly with clarity and persuasiveness, and which Harriet Beecher soon adopted. As his literary platform, Hall advocated cheerfulness, morality, and regionalism. He was an outstanding defender of fiction, and with rollicking good humor that sometimes became biting satire he opened endless vistas of promise for the young writers of the West.

Hall was also, as his references to the fair sex clearly show, a chivalrous admirer of women writers. By accepting their work for his magazines he proved how highly he esteemed, to quote him, "those attractive attributes of the female pen, and of the female heart, pure morality and delicate sentiment."[6] All of these attitudes were to be carried over from the *Illinois Monthly* to the *Western Monthly*, the only difference being that under its new name the publication was expected to be, as indeed it was, bigger and better.

Harriet Beecher, newly arrived from New England, could hardly have known immediately that to become a contributor to the new magazine she would need to exhibit in her writing cheerful energy, local color, and refined morality. She need not have remained long in ignorance, for Hall was his own press agent. In the January, 1833, issue the opening note "To the Reader" would have been especially interesting to the prospective contributor. "We live in a country and an age, governed by moral influence," was a proposition to which the youngest Miss Beecher would murmur a hearty assent. "The literature of our country has never exerted the influence to which it is entitled," was another proposition to set one thinking. How was the *Western Monthly* to meet this problem? Explained the editor, who made a special appeal to educators: "Although devoted chiefly to elegant literature, it has always been our wish and endeavor, to render it useful, by making it the medium for disseminating valuable information and pure moral principles" (I [1833], 2-3). Without this definite endorsement of virtue, Hall might never have enlisted the interest of the Beechers. He had appealed, that is, to their dominant interest.

Satisfactory as his opening note was, Hall followed it with an even more significant and suggestive article entitled "American Literature." The emphasis was partly patriotic but mainly financial. Mrs. Stowe's later professional attitude toward her writing—namely, to get all she could from it—was encouraged, if not actually instigated, by Hall. The English people, he pointed out, paid their writers much more generously than Americans did, and he complained especially that native book publishers rejected native works because they objected to paying authors' royalties. "The American writer must give his labor for nothing," he protested, "or be driven from the field by this disadvantageous competition." To improve the condition of American writers he urged, in particular, greater financial support for American periodicals. "Patronage should *come first*," he insisted; then literary journals could afford to pay their writers better (I [1833], 8-9).

Harriet must have sat down immediately to do some writing, for her first contribution, "Modern Uses of Language," appeared in the third issue. Signed simply "B," it was attributed to Catherine Beecher, though it was Harriet's work (CES, 69). While the elder sister took public credit, the younger found what was more important and valuable: an introduction to the art of pleasing editors.

Not much need be said about this light essay. In it Harriet maintained whimsically that the modern uses of language are to conceal either ideas or the lack of them. She drew her examples of obscurity from Milton and Dugald Stewart and her examples of empty clichés from undesignated minor writers. Her motto, chosen with inevitable cleverness, was Hamlet's "Words, words, words!"

The next high spot in the *Western Monthly* is to be found in the sixth issue of June, 1833. A brief review, much the briefest for the month, it can be quoted here completely:

> Primary Geography for Children, on an improved plan, with twelve maps, and numerous engravings. By C. and H. Beecher, Principals of the Western Female Institute. Cincinnati: Corey and Fairbank.
>
> This is very capital little book. The authoresses are accomplished young ladies, who have made the tuition of youth their study and business for several years, and who unite to a competent knowledge of the subject, an intimate acquaintance with the best modes of teaching children. Writing books

for children is one of the most difficult, and surely one of the most useful branches of authorship. We most cordially recommend this, as a successful effort in this noble field.

The issue of September, 1833, offered A PREMIUM OF FIFTY DOLLARS—all in capital letters—for a story and a similar one for an essay. In December the essay appeared as scheduled. "Themes for Western Fiction," by Isaac Appleton Jewett. Since it gave Hall his own ideas back again, he commended it highly. At the same time, he extended the story contest, since no worthy entries had been received. When a decision was finally reached, Harriet Beecher's winning story was used to open the issue of April, 1834. While the award for the short-story contest was being held back, Harriet's story "Isabelle and her Sister Kate, and their Cousin" appeared in the February, 1834, issue of the magazine (II [1834], 72-75). This story, signed "May," preceded by two months the prize-winning "New England Sketch" which has usually been considered her first published story. Nor can there be any doubt of the authorship, as the following abstract will show.

Miss Isabelle was very beautiful and popular; her young sister Kate was plain but nice. She excelled in "being happy," in spite of her social eclipse. "She had a world of sprightliness, a deal of simplicity and affection, with a dash of goodnatured shrewdness," and she adored her elder sister. The girls are visited by their cousin Edward, a valedictorian. The whole town gossips about his affection for the grand Isabelle, but he is really in love with quiet, retiring Kate. "No, Miss Catharine, it's you!" he finally blurts out. The last paragraph reads: "Poor little Kate! it was her turn to look at the cotton balls, and to exhibit symptoms of scarlet fever; and while she is thinking what to say next, you may read the next piece in the magazine."

The similarity of these situations to later stories by Mrs. Stowe—especially "Love *versus* Law"—does not need to be pointed out. The sketch was also reprinted five years later, under Harriet's name, in the Cincinnati *Chronicle*, though never in any of her books.

Following the prize story in April, Hall used her "Frankness" in May, attributing it to "A Lady," and in July "Sister Mary," with her initials. These three, reprinted in *The Mayflower* of

1843, show to what extent the young writer was developing a recognizable and commercially valuable "style" or manner of her own. The part played by James Hall in developing this manner deserves specific mention. For a short time he was to her what Lowell became after the founding of the *Atlantic*: a restraining influence upon her sentimentality, and an encouragement to her better qualities of observation and humor. For example, he could review Mrs. Sigourney's *Sketches* (1834) favorably, "it is calculated to do good," but he could also make the reservation that "the sentiment is excellent in its way, but there is a little more of it than suits our taste" (II [1834], 445). This is precisely the counsel Harriet Beecher needed, and her work would have been better if Hall's influence had lasted longer.[7]

Of much less importance than the *Western Monthly Magazine*, but still essential to an appreciation of Mrs. Stowe's early literary activities, is her relationship to two other Cincinnati publications, weekly papers, the *Chronicle* and the *Journal*. The case for the *Chronicle* is stated by its one-time editor, E. D. Mansfield: "Mrs. Stowe, then Miss Beecher, published her first stories in it."[8] The explanation of this error is that these "first stories" were *reprinted* in the *Chronicle*, and that editor Mansfield, after forty-five years, did not remember quite correctly.

At various dates from May 3, 1834, the *Chronicle* reprinted Mrs. Stowe's stories. The prize tale, the first to be so honored, took the whole of page one and half of page two; it was perhaps the longest contribution ever to appear in a single issue of the *Chronicle*. "It is a beauteous tale," wrote the editor, "and bears the stamp of genius." Later in the same month the *Chronicle* reprinted "Frankness" without the author's name. Four years later, under Mansfield's editorship, "Frankness" was again reprinted, to be followed by "Cousin William" and "Isabelle and her Sister Kate, and their Cousin." After it had grown into a daily, the *Chronicle* continued the policy of reprinting Mrs. Stowe's tales.

By this simple means Mrs. Stowe's work became known to every citizen of Cincinnati, establishing her as a literary light second only to the older Mrs. Caroline Hentz. By implication, the *Chronicle* put her on a par with other writers who were often reprinted. Of these the *Chronicle's* favorites were Mrs. Lydia Maria Child, T. S. Arthur, Miss Catharine Maria Sedgwick, and above all Mrs. Lydia Huntley Sigourney. To be on terms of equality with these writers, even locally, was, in the 1830's and 1840's, to be well on the way towards the literary heights. Newspaper readers would have admitted that Mrs. Stowe was at least distinctly promising. The *Chronicle* reprints helped her to gain this reputation.

Her connection with the *Journal and Western Luminary* was closer, though here also the literary importance of the connection was slight. The *Journal*, a weekly Presbyterian paper, was deeply devoted to Lyman Beecher and Lane Seminary; and it was also on close terms with the New York *Evangelist*, one of Mrs. Stowe's other markets. While the *Journal's* editor, T. Brainerd, was out of town at the general assembly of his church, his place was taken as editor *pro tem* by young Henry Ward Beecher. The year was 1836, and as Professor Stowe was also away on a mission to investigate European education, his young wife was free to assist her brother with the *Journal*. How much she assisted him is a question, since her writing for the paper was without by-line and not personal enough to reveal her authorship.

III *Contributions to Eastern Publications*

From the Cincinnati *Journal* to the New York *Evangelist* was a greater step geographically than culturally, for both were staunchly Presbyterian. The *Evangelist* accurately described itself as "Devoted to Revivals, Doctrinal Discussion and Religious Intelligence Generally." It reprinted matter from the Cincinnati *Journal*, thereby repaying the *Journal's* compliment in reprinting from it. The medium of Harriet Beecher's introduction to it is thus easily seen. She was led to it by her family, rather than introduced by a literary outsider like James Hall.

The *Evangelist* also ran a department of "Secular Intelligence" and used nonsectarian material of a moralizing tendency by writers like Mrs. Sigourney. Harriet's first contribution (1835), initialed "E.B.," was a temperance tale entitled "Uncle Enoch," a plotless but not pointless narrative of how a benevolent deacon induced people to sign the abstainer's pledge. To add that the kind deacon had three lovely daughters who helped in his work is to complete the story.

Sixteen years later, in 1851, almost on the verge of *Uncle Tom's Cabin*, Mrs. Stowe was still writing for the *Evangelist*. During the intervening years her offerings had been neither frequent nor significant, but some were reprinted in her collections of 1843 and 1855. Of the unreprinted pieces several dealt with the need of giving money to religious causes. One spoke of the possibility of spiritualism, a subject of great interest to her later. Others presented, mildly but firmly, her family's objections to the Roman Catholics. In addition to these strictly religious papers, a few spread more widely, like two articles on "Literary Epidemics."

Meanwhile, as if in emulation of Mrs. Sigourney—who stopped counting after she had published 2000 pieces in periodicals— Mrs. Stowe was releasing her work through a surprisingly large number of magazines and gift annuals. Mrs. Sigourney's own *Religious Souvenir* opened its pages to her. So did the *Christian Keepsake*, which numbered among its contributors Mrs. Sigourney, Mrs. Sarah Josepha Hale, and Catherine Beecher. *The Gift*, as has been mentioned, printed "Love *versus* Law" under the editorship of Miss Leslie, and somebody was so struck by another of Mrs. Stowe's tales, "Mark Meridan," that it was published as part of a book, in company with a story by Miss Leslie herself and two by T. S. Arthur.[9] The august *Token*, the aristocrat of the annuals, printed one of her most characteristic early stories, "The Yankee Girl," which was never reprinted but is interesting because it foreshadows—in the clash between a sturdy New England maiden and a questionable aristocrat— a situation used in *The Minister's Wooing* and in *Oldtown Folks*. Her work also appeared in the *Banquet*, the *Christian Souvenir*, and the *Violet*, as well as, later, in T. S. Arthur's *Temperance Offering* for 1853. In the complete list of her contributions to the annuals, industrious marketing is shown as well as industrious writing.

Godey's Lady's Book, another of her regular markets, made much the same appeal as many of the annuals. Though it published work by some important authors—Emerson, Poe, Irving—its mainstays were such tried and true minor figures as Mrs. Sigourney, who was also a member of the editorial board; Mrs. Frances Osgood; Mrs. Caroline Hentz of Cincinnati; Miss Leslie; Mrs. M. St. Leon Loud; Miss Hannah Gould; and Mr. T. S. Arthur. Among Mrs. Stowe's efforts never reclaimed from this publication were a moral tale about a spoiled girl, "The Only Daughter"; a skit, "Olympiana," in which Greek deities were modernized in the style of 1840; and a secular poem translated from Goethe.

A complete analysis of Mrs. Stowe's commercial writing preceding *Uncle Tom's Cabin* would be more wearisome than profitable. She could write as carelessly as her more complaisant editors permitted, or as carefully as her more exacting ones demanded. "The Yankee Girl" is as superior to "The Seamstress" as the *Token* is to the *Religious Souvenir*. Morally, she never wrote against her conscience; and she never needed to appear in an unworthy light, for her editors were fully as particular as she was. The product she sold was wholesome entertainment; her public, the masses.

Yet however careless her writing, she never reached the extremes of sentimentality of some of her contemporaries. In the same *Religious Souvenir* (1840) with "The Seamstress" is a story in which the sinfulness of giving a social party is wept over as if it were the destruction of Pompeii. Mrs. Stowe was never to equal such absurdity. "The Seamstress" is, after all, a worthy if wordy plea for the unfortunate that has at least some connection with wholesome living. As the best of these sketches show, she had learned a valuable lesson: to be freshly observant and moral but with flashes of Yankee wit and frontier humor.

This salutary principle was, however, in conflict with another which might be attributed to the *Evangelist* or, further back, to sister Catherine's pedagogy: the desire to do good sometimes refused to be kept within intelligent limits. The annuals allowed her to run wild, confirming her habit of easy, conventional writing and challenging neither her keenness of expression nor her subtlety of thought. "The Tea-Rose," a special favorite with Mrs. Hale, is only one example of many aesthetic misfortunes.[10]

IV *Young Mrs. Stowe's Type of Writer*

Now that the details have been set down, one wants to consider the picture they make. Just how far did all this writing take young Mrs. Stowe, and where did it leave her? Isn't there a long jump between these trifles and *Uncle Tom's Cabin*? To answer the first of these questions—for the jump to *Uncle Tom's Cabin* is not nearly so long as Eliza's jump across the Ohio River—this early writing gave Mrs. Stowe membership in a distinct group of woman writers of the time with whom she never ceased to have relationship.

When Harriet Beecher decided to write professionally she had three distinct possibilities to explore. The heady intellectual woman writer who was to appear a little later, in George Eliot and Mrs. Humphrey Ward, was represented only by Margaret Fuller; and the independent experimenter, like Emily Dickinson or Gertrude Stein, was still farther in the future. Lacking these, the early nineteenth century offered only the types of the sublimely epic, the passionately romantic, and the piously domestic.[11] Harriet specialized almost entirely in the third of these.

Among women writers on the grand scale, of whom the Cincinnati representative was Mrs. Caroline Hentz, the most outstanding was Mrs. Maria Gowen Brooks, known as Maria del Occidente, whose biblical epic *Zophiël* was lavishly praised by Rufus Griswold, Robert Southey, and Charles Lamb. Amid her rich rhymes and a battery of poetic names like Egla and Meles, Mrs. Brooks's admiring contemporaries found beauties equal to Dante and Milton. Mrs. Louisa J. Hall, another of the type admiringly represented in Griswold's *Female Poets of America*, was noted for her *Miriam*, a poetic drama of early Christianity.

Upon such sublimity Mrs. Stowe sternly, if perhaps reluctantly, turned her back. Her childhood tragedy of *Cleon*, which introduced the cruelties of Nero, had been indeed just such a play as Mrs. Hall's *Miriam* or Mrs. Elizabeth Oakes-Smith's *The Roman Tribute*; and the record states that she abandoned it with sadness. In her professional days, though many magazines welcomed such flights into baseless grandeur, she was seldom tempted. A sketch in *The May Flower* of 1855, a description of Christ's procession to the cross, is one of her few attempts in this vein. An epic vision from the *Evangelist,* "Now we see through a glass darkly," was never salvaged. There are passages in her novels, however, that recall such "grace and godlike majesty" as Mrs. Hall's; in fact, her Italian novel *Agnes of Sorrento* was planned too nearly in the same vein for its own good.

As romantic passion meant so much less to her than sublimity, Mrs. Stowe was less tempted by the lures of feminine eroticism. Critics and magazine editors might be susceptible to melodious lovelorn maidens, but not Calvin Stowe's wife. In Byron and Mme. de Staël she had encountered wayward sentiments, but she kept them, when she could, for such misled, pathetic creatures as the light-headed girls in *The Pearl of Orr's Island* and in *Pink and White Tyranny.* From the beginning she shunned girlish love-longing for the soberer sentiments of the Christian wife and mother.

This last was, though not the only, by far the most popular temperament among early nineteenth-century literary women, the condemned mob of scribblers who goaded Hawthorne into profanity. Mrs. Sigourney and Miss Sedgwick were no more perfect in their pious resignation than Miss Hannah Gould, the housekeeper poetess, a steady contributor to the *Western Monthly.* But the ones most worthy of observation, as showing on a large scale the fine flower of the tradition in which Mrs. Stowe worked, were the younger women: Susan Warner, author of *The Wide, Wide World,* the great success of 1850; and Mrs. Elizabeth Prentiss, author of *Stepping Heavenward,* a lesser success of 1869. Miss Warner prepared the way for Mrs. Stowe's success, and Mrs. Prentiss, entirely without literary encouragement, carried religious emotionalism to its ultimate extreme.

As far as *The Wide, Wide World* is concerned, its account is easily reckoned; for pathos and piety were the leading ingredients of this lengthy account of a troubled girlhood. Sent from New York City into the country by her dying mother, Ellen Montgomery suffered under a harsh but not inhuman paternal aunt; found godly friends; and, after becoming an orphan, repeated the round of suffering and friendship under the affectionate but rough guardianship of a maternal uncle. A sweet and studious girl, she grew sweeter and more studious through adversity, finally becoming a true Christian on Mrs. Stowe's own model, earnest and charitable, strict with herself but tender toward others.

Stepping Heavenward, which was published in book form in 1869 after serialization in a church paper, is an almost classic distillation of nineteenth-century sentimental piety. In form, the book is the journal of Katherine Mortimer; beginning in 1831, when the girl is sixteen years old, it relates her growth into grace, as marriage and suffering transform the rebellious imp of nature into a saintly mother. The reader's last glimpse of her is as a bedridden invalid. The old family physician is visiting her:

> "Ah, these lovely children are explained now," he said.
> "Do you really think," I asked, "that it has been good for my children to have a feeble, afflicted mother?"
> "Yes, I really think so. A disciplined mother—disciplined children."
> This comforting thought is one of the last drops in a cup of felicity already full.[12]

To this extreme of self-abnegation Harriet Beecher Stowe herself might have come had not the success of *Uncle Tom's Cabin* given her a new direction. Her early work that has been surveyed in this chapter was as passive, almost as gentle, as Mrs. Prentiss'. A little longer social obscurity was all she needed to decide that the life of the spirit, without worldly prosperity, was best.

How then did Mrs. Stowe escape? Stylistically, she never wholly escaped, but emotionally she escaped through an act of bold rebellion. When she began writing *Uncle Tom's Cabin* she was forty years old, sick, poor, and overworked. In many of her moods she was completely miserable. A lifetime of work had brought only the necessity for more work. She was a slave.

At this moment chance intervened to help her. The literary stage had been prepared for sentimentalism by such writers as Mrs. Sigourney and, more recently, by Miss Warner. Mrs. Stowe herself had learned the trade of writing. History—the Congress of the United States and the Supreme Court of the land—now miraculously provided the occasion of the Fugitive Slave Law, by which sentimentalism could be attached to a burning issue. Her resentment toward the repressive influences in her own life, which she never dared admit to herself, attached itself to the symbol of the black race.

Into *Uncle Tom's Cabin*, therefore, Mrs. Stowe was able to pour her whole life—everything she had learned about writing and everything she had learned about living. The sentiment of the annuals and gift books was there; the unction of the New York *Evangelist;* the lesson of sharp observation learned from James Hall. It was all a wonderful summary of her past life, completely dwarfing anything she had done before, yet built inevitably from her experiences as a writer and a Beecher.

CHAPTER 3

Uncle Tom's Cabin

I *Designs*

AS THE CENTRAL MOMENT in Mrs. Stowe's life, the publication of *Uncle Tom's Cabin* has received comparatively detailed scrutiny from her biographers. Before the book's success, she was poor and unknown; after it, she was rich and famous. The contrast is pleasant enough to tempt a lingering treatment. In her developing literary life, *Uncle Tom's Cabin* is equally important. Before it, her work had been tentative and fragmentary; after it she was free, as the greatest of American women writers, to write as she wanted and on as large a scale as she cared. She no longer asked to get manuscripts published, for she was begged for more contributions than she could find time to write. Here again the contrast is a pleasant one. Between these two stages lies the little matter of the two-volume novel; and if the discussion seems rather long-drawn out, the reader can console himself by recalling that it is at least much shorter than Mrs. Stowe's story.

For some technical purposes, the substance of *Uncle Tom's Cabin* might be summed up in a paragraph, the design is so easily stated. The book is one of those Victorian novels in which, according to a common practice, the adventures of two groups of characters are alternated to give an inclusive picture of society and to provide a variety of emotional appeal. In *Uncle Tom's Cabin* the contrasting groups commence as slaves in the border state of Kentucky. Tom, a middle-aged, intelligent black man, is sold southward down the river. His experiences, forming the main plot, introduce numerous types of slaveholders and their human possessions. In the second plot Eliza, a young yellow-skinned matron and one of Tom's fellow slaves, is the central figure. As she flees to Canada, various characters are introduced as typical of the abolitionist enthusiasts along the underground railway.

For the greater part, the two distinct plots are developed with an almost architectural balance that extends to the obviously strong contrast between the refuge of Eliza's party in free Ontario and the last solitary misery of Tom in despotic Louisiana. This design is easily kept in mind; and, for a clear conception of the story as such, one need add only a few other characters, without many more details than might appear as notes with the dramatis personae of a printed play.

In the approximate order of their appearance the reader meets:

Mr. Shelby, Tom's first owner, a Kentucky gentleman forced by economic necessity to sell Tom in spite of the humanitarian objections of Mrs. Shelby and the affection of Master Shelby.

Haley, a crude slave dealer who buys Tom, and also Eliza's little boy, for resale; his friend Loker, a more brutal slave dealer than Haley.

Slaves on the Shelby plantation, including Tom's wife Chloe, and Sam, a clever rascal.

George Harris, Eliza's husband, a talented, nearly white slave on a neighboring plantation, who also escapes to Canada and eventual reunion with his wife and child.

Workers on the underground railway: specifically, Mrs. Bird and her husband, state senator in Ohio; various Quakers; and others necessary to the action but not appearing throughout the story.

Mr. Augustine St. Clare, Tom's second kind owner, prevented by sudden death from freeing Tom; his sister from Vermont, Miss Ophelia, the voice of righteousness according to old Calvinistic standards; his wife, a cruel and vain Southern aristocrat; their saintly daughter Eva.

Slaves in the St. Clare household, notably Topsy, a vivacious youngster about the age of Eva.

Simon Legree, Tom's third owner, viciousness incarnate, defiler of women, torturer of the helpless, and murderer of Tom.

Slaves on Legree's plantation, malicious or sodden representations of the worst slavery can do.

Although the skeleton of the story is now before the reader, the substance of the book eludes such tabulation, for the power and the individuality of *Uncle Tom's Cabin* depend less on this conventional literary kind of material than on the author's assumptions and suppressed conflicts. Actions and characters, whatever they may be, are bent to satisfy the inner compulsions of Lyman Beecher's daughter and Calvin Stowe's wife. Uncle Tom, a passive suffering Christ, and Eliza, a mother in revolt, are thin disguises of the author. The passion with which she presents them, a half-expression, projects personal problems without the true objectification of art, but with an emotional power that was overwhelming in the midst of the national crisis of the 1850's.

II *The Opening Chapters*

To turn to the opening pages of *Uncle Tom's Cabin* is to be introduced to a lady with an acute sense of propriety: "For convenience' sake, we have said, hitherto, two *gentlemen*. One of the parties, however, when critically examined, did not seem strictly speaking to come under the species."[1] Continuing with the description of the questionable "party" drinking wine in a well-furnished dining parlor in the town of P—— in Kentucky, one soon suspects the author of a distaste for the fellow. He was overdressed, she complains, wore too much jewelry, spoke ungrammatically, and indulged in "various profane expressions, which not even the desire to be graphic in our account shall induce us to transcribe."

As the objectionable Haley sits talking with Mr. Shelby and drinking his reluctant host's wine and brandy, the narrative proper is promptly begun by the mention of Tom, not yet avuncular, whose virtues are extolled by the master to the prospective purchaser. Eliza's child, rushing into the room and performing an impromptu minstrel act with singing, dancing, and mimicking, is soon followed by his mother, a quadroon of about twenty-five whose ravishing beauty draws justified praise from the businesslike slave dealer.

As these unusual persons appear, what fiction addict can resist curiosity over their futures? Before he knows the direction, he is eager to set out; no matter how long the serial, he will be held fast. With economy and skill—the author was never to create so neat an opening again—the drama has already begun, for dismayed Mother Eliza has recognized the slave trader's mission. The terror which is one of the dominant notes of the book is clearly indicated in an impassioned interview between her and her mistress.

Meanwhile the crass Haley has expressed what Mrs. Stowe consistently regarded as the most dangerous heresy about the Negroes. "These critters ain't like white folks, you know," he explains, a denial of humanity to the slaves that was anathema to Mrs. Stowe (6). Throughout the first chapter Mrs. Stowe forces Haley to damn himself through his own speeches, only to weaken the effect by permitting Mr. Shelby to damn him in soliloquy. In the art of fiction, it soon becomes apparent, Mrs. Stowe has not left behind her *Lady's Book* mannerisms; and the *National Era* appropriately followed *Uncle Tom's Cabin* with one of its many serials by Mrs. E. D. E. N. Southworth.

In the second chapter, Eliza and her husband become the center of attention. The young colored man, to whom is ascribed mechanical genius equal to Eli Whitney's, is shown to be the victim of an envious master's hatred:

Yes, Eliza, it's all misery, misery! My life is bitter as wormwood; the very life is burning out of me. I'm a poor, miserable, forlorn drudge. . . . My master! and who made him my master? That's what I think of,—what right has he to me? I'm a man as much as he is. I'm a better man than he is. I know more about business than he does. . . (18).

In spite of this emphatic preparation, the foreshadowed escape is transferred to Eliza. The spectacular climax, Eliza's wild leap out of her pursuers' clutches and escape across the Ohio River, is well known—somewhat inaccurately, for there were no bloodhounds in the original, only in lavish productions of George Aiken's play. In Mrs. Stowe's words:

She caught her child and sprang down the steps. . . . In
that dizzy moment her feet to her scarce seemed to touch
the ground, and a moment brought her to the water's edge.
Right on behind they came; and, nerved with strength such
as God gives only to the desperate, with one wild cry and
flying leap, she vaulted sheer over the turbid current by the
shore, on to the rafter of ice beyond. It was a desperate leap,—
impossible to anything but madness and despair. . . . The
huge green fragment of ice on which she alighted pitched
and creaked as her weight came on it, but she stayed there
not a moment. With wild cries and desperate energy she
leaped to another and still another cake; stumbling,—leaping,
—slipping,—springing upwards again! Her shoes are gone,—
her stockings cut from her feet,—while blood marked every
step; but she saw nothing, felt nothing, till dimly, as in a dream,
she saw the Ohio side, and a man helping her up the bank
(73-75).

That is the account in a page, a score of lines in which Eliza,
the brave young mother, was immortalized.

The immediate result of Eliza's desperate escape, Haley's
conversation with his friend Loker, an even more inhuman
slave dealer, and the latter's grotesque companion, Marks,
affords another excellent opportunity for Mrs. Stowe's most
persuasive device, the self-condemnation of characters who act
against God's will. In the cynical stories told so glibly by these
debased traders, there is a perverted humor that sinks deep
into the underground passages of human nature.

III *The Central Chapters: St. Clare and Miss Ophelia*

How packed with life and action the opening chapters of
Uncle Tom's Cabin are! Carelessly strung together for periodical
publication, unlikely and exaggerated, they still show one
essential gift of the storyteller: an ability to arouse attention.
The early reader, not caring about Mrs. Stowe's private problems, merely wanted to know what happened to Tom and
Eliza after they left Kentucky; and, as he pressed on, greater
thrills than before were in store for him. In the central division
of the book, Tom's life with his new masters is contrasted
with the protection the refugees find among the Quakers,

examples of stout-hearted Northern abolitionists. Chronological exactness is discarded here, for while Tom is abiding two years and more with his kind masters, Eliza and George do not reach Canada, toward which they are hurrying at full speed, until after the death of St. Clare. Their arrival in Ontario immediately precedes the chapter presaging Tom's Louisiana martyrdom.

In the St. Clare family, inhabitants of a picturesque mansion in New Orleans, Mrs. Stowe portrayed slaveholders at their best. A kind master, a heavenly young mistress, a puzzled Vermont aunt—these line up on the credit side; and against them is only a spoiled daughter of wealth, unthinkingly heartless but too indolent to be aggressively cruel. Tom adapted himself to his new owners, for they had almost as sound an appreciation of his virtues as he of theirs. In particular was he idolized by Eva, whose life he had saved by hauling her from the Mississippi, a river which might have flowed, as Mrs. Stowe described it, straight from the exotic pages of Chateaubriand's *Atala* but has never elsewhere appeared to human eyes. Knowing how fortunate he was, Tom could have been completely happy had he not been separated from his family and held in slavery. His existence lay in a calm before the final storm precipitated by St. Clare's sudden death.

Meanwhile, shrewdly holding Simon Legree offstage, Mrs. Stowe delivered her keenest and fairest attacks upon Negro slavery, the supposed subject of her book. As usual, she put her criticism into the mouth of one of her characters. Of all the creations serving this purpose, Augustine St. Clare is the most engaging and the most convincing. A worldling, he has no serious vices, his lack of purpose seeming rather to aid him in viewing life objectively. He is a man who likes to talk, who enjoys being amusing and shocking, and whose principal conversational weapon is a straightforward honesty that his slower-witted auditors mistake for paradox. He is a good fellow, Mrs. Stowe would have her readers realize, as she apologizes profusely for his frivolity, accounting for it by his unfortunate marriage and his loss, at only thirteen, of his saintly mother. Misfortune's child, he is neither hypocrite nor fool. Mrs. Stowe compares him to Thomas Moore, to Goethe, and to Lord Byron.

With Miss Ophelia, the old-fashioned Calvinist aunt, as interlocutor, St. Clare chatters on at length. At the prim spinster's discomfort over the familiarities permitted between Tom and Eva, he laughs:

> I know the feeling among some of you northerners well enough. Not that there is a particle of virtue in our not having it; but custom with us does what Christianity ought to do,—obliterates the feeling of personal prejudice. I have often noticed, in my travels north, how much stronger this was with you than with us. You loathe them as you would a snake or a toad, yet you are indignant at their wrongs. You would not have them abused; but you don't want to have anything to do with them yourselves. You would send them to Africa, out of your sight and smell, and then send a missionary or two to do up all the self-denial of elevating them compendiously. Isn't that it? (208)

These points were well scored. In Mrs. Stowe's own home she might easily have observed the Yankee prejudice against blacks, and the proposal for colonization had also been seriously advocated by the Beechers.

In the more serious mood which seizes him upon occasion, St. Clare expresses strangely proletarian judgments on wage-slavery: "Look at the high and the low, all the world over, and it's the same story,—the lower class used up, body, soul, and spirit for the good of the upper. It is so in England; it is so everywhere" (249). Or this: "The slave-owner can whip his refractory slave to death,—the capitalist can starve him to death. As to family security it is hard to say which is the worst,—to have one's children sold, or see them starve to death at home" (268). Or this striking parallel to the then recent *Communist Manifesto* of Marx and Engels: "One thing is certain,—that there is a mustering among the masses, the world over; and there is a *dies irae* coming on, sooner or later. The same thing is working in Europe, in England, and in this country" (270-71).

Incredible as it may seem, the sense of social economic responsibility implied in St. Clare's speeches was utterly foreign to Mrs. Stowe's thought. Chattel slavery she regarded as iniquitous, and wage slavery as free choice. Never for a moment did she consider the application of St. Clare's ideas to the

North. She could denounce the capitalists of monarchical England—some of the English proved unpleasantly sensitive on this point—but she honestly did not know that there existed New England mills in which laborers were working for starvation pay. Quite to the contrary, she held up these factories in the *First Geography for Children* (1855) as special evidence of God's favor.[2]

In St. Clare's speeches Mrs. Stowe let him run away from her, and she barely succeeded in bringing him back into the circle of her own ideas by turning his thoughts heavenward. Recalling the millennium promised by his blessed mother, he staggers safely back into the Beecher theology and away from the dangers of political radicalism. Unfortunately for Tom, St. Clare saved was also St. Clare dead. The man's soul was in heaven, but Tom was left to the mercy of his frivolous, heartless widow.

IV *Black Topsy, Evangeline, and Simon Legree*

If St. Clare's role is profitable fictional property, Topsy's is a gold mine of humor. The wayward slave girl, endowed with the supershowmanship of her race, is equipped by nature to step onto the stage with Christy's Ethiopian Minstrels, who were not only a metropolitan sensation in 1851-52 but had also appeared in Cincinnati in 1846 and 1847. A challenge to Miss Ophelia's power of discipline, Topsy is used to point the true moral of the tale—that love is above law; for only Eva's superhuman love started Topsy upon the path towards decency.

As little Evangeline was admittedly a miracle, it is not strange that the solution of the slavery problem looked far, far away to Mrs. Stowe. Since proper relations between the races could be attained only through personal love like Eva's, which was as inclusive as that of Jesus, the problem was a religious one. All the more scandalous, therefore, was the refusal of the churches to do their duty. To be a reformer in those days, said Mrs. Stowe, it was necessary to be unchristian, for churches were godless and ministers weak and hypocritical. Not everybody liked this interpretation of the churches, and Mrs. Stowe needed later to defend herself against charges of impiety.

By this middle section of her book Mrs. Stowe had not yet solved to her own satisfaction all the mysteries of Negro slavery. From the beginning of its serial publication she held for absolute legal freedom as a minimum, pointing out upon one occasion that George Harris held up his head, speaking and moving like a different man as soon as he regarded himself as "free," though at the time he was still doubtful of his eventual safety. Slavery, in its criminal regard of human souls as mere property, was, she thought, a relation different in kind from the woes of ordinary life. Uncle Tom took issue with his creator upon this point, for she showed his basic tragedy to be that he was a true Christian among the heathen; and he himself rightly regarded slavery as only one added indignity. A certain "unfashionable old book," from which he read solely in the New Testament, separated him more completely from his fellow men than either color or servitude.

Tom wanted his freedom, to be sure, as ardently as Mrs. Stowe wanted it for him; but he preferred slavery and martyrdom to dishonorable flight. He was a black Christ shaming a Yankee Satan. And so, to provide the catharsis of a soul-stirring conclusion, Legree was provided—the blackest-hearted villain that ever dishonored his fair New England origin.

In considering the three sections into which the book is divided, it can be observed that the first, in its description of the Shelby estate, enriches the tale with verisimilitude, for Mrs. Stowe had been as far south as Kentucky; the second, in Topsy and St. Clare, with wit and humor; and the third, in Legree, with terror. In Eliza's wild flight, a similar terror appears at the opening of the story, a dramatic foreboding of the powerful conclusion.

As a work of troubled imagination, there is much to be said for *Uncle Tom's Cabin*. For the episode of Legree particularly, the secluded plantation in the wilderness, the grotesque and cruel inhabitants, the pitiable victims, and the intervention of supernatural powers offer material that neither Anne Radcliffe nor Monk Lewis could have used to better advantage than did Mrs. Stowe. When Tom nobly suffers martyrdom, lingering only long enough to bid farewell to his young master from Kentucky, it is not strange that, in 1852, tears fell upon the pages of the *National Era*.

Even so, when the book was completed, its success was not nearly so assured as the usual accounts suggest. Abolitionist literature was frankly boycotted by many publishers, and Mrs. Stowe secured book publication only after difficult negotiations with an unestablished publisher who would have preferred her to run a large share of the financial risk. If she would contribute five hundred dollars, he would pay her a royalty of fifty per cent.[3] Not accepting this gamble was a mistake for which she suffered the cruelest of penalties. The sales, commencing strong, swelled into thousands and hundreds of thousands. The young publisher's speculation was amply rewarded.

So was Mrs. Stowe, but her meager ten per cent royalty provided another durable complaint against fate, when she thought of the rejected fifty per cent. In the book's success she soon forgot the willingness with which she would have sold her rights for enough money, as her husband had stated his original ambition for her, to buy a new silk dress.[4]

V *Sources*

The triumph of *Uncle Tom's Cabin* was more astonishing to the author than she could afterward explain. Her final suggestion, that she had not written it but had taken it in dictation from God, satisfied her in her old age. Before reaching this solution, she had been inclined to take most of the credit herself, with an assist from Henry Ward's promise to scatter her still unwritten words thick as the leaves of Vallombrosa. Or perhaps, as she believed in 1870, she had been driven to write it, like her other books, "by the necessity of making some income for family expenses" (AF, 327). Nor could she decide exactly where or when she had started to write and whether the death of Uncle Tom was the first or the last part of the book to be set down.

Among the least convincing of her attempts to explain the mystery is the suggestion, later accepted in her son's official biography, that the novel was slowly evolved, thought over as a long-planned contribution to the abolition movement. Against the credibility of this view one need only recall that in *The Mayflower* sketches of 1843 slavery and abolition had received not so much as passing mention, an oversight corrected in the enlarged edition after the success of *Uncle Tom's Cabin.* During the long years of antislavery activity in which she did no writing for the cause, Mrs. Stowe may well have been personally disturbed; but she remained socially unawakened and publicly uncommitted. The need for independence as individual fulfillment had been her personal problem, but Negro slavery was a different matter: she was a retarded convert to abolition, avoiding it in her writing until the Northern moral revolt against the Fugitive Slave Law of 1850.

In contrast to uncertain memories and undocumented claims, authentic sources for parts of *Uncle Tom's Cabin* have been identified. The autobiography of Josiah Henson, an escaped slave who later became famous as the original of Uncle Tom, is one of these. Henson, a genial soul, godly and respectful, was enough like Uncle Tom in appearance and character to overwhelm his lecture audiences with his similarities to that famous man. In her preface to the 1878 edition of her novel Mrs. Stowe specifically mentioned her visits to the antislavery rooms in Boston to consult certain "documents"—her term for abolitionist pamphlets—including the life of Josiah Henson, that of Lewis Clarke, and Theodore Weld's *Slavery As It Is.* She knew Henson's book well, and there are also records of visits from Henson at Boston and Andover. His idealistic character was congenial to her, many of his traits finding their way into her depiction of Tom.

Undoubted as his services to her were, their exact content is disputable. In one respect these two people were alike: for while Henson was inclined to exaggerate his helpfulness, Mrs. Stowe considered that her generosity was ample in a reference to his published autobiography as "an exemplification of the truth of the character of her Uncle Tom." According to Henson, however, he supplied her with the originals of George Harris and Eliza, his particular friends; of Topsy, as near like a certain Dinah on his old plantation as one pea to another; of Simon Legree, in the person of Bryce Litton, "who broke my arms and marred me for life"; and also of St. Clare and Eva, in the persons of a Mr. St. Clair Young and his daughter.[5]

Except for George Harris, Henson was mistaken in these identifications. To the limited degree in which Eliza was drawn from life she was either a fugitive whom Calvin Stowe and Henry Ward Beecher had helped, or she was, according to another family explanation, the subject of an account in an antislavery paper. The human original of Topsy was a colored girl, Celeste by name, known to the family in Cincinnati. The character of Legree, which seems to have been both fathered and mothered by writers of melodramas, is said to have been sketched for her by her brother Charles, who had been a clerk in Louisiana.[6]

To Theodore Weld, her debt was greater than to Josiah Henson, and perhaps greater than she understood. Weld, whom she had known many years before, had been a brilliant student at Lane Seminary during Lyman Beecher's presidency. An abolitionist even in 1834, Weld had been threatened with expulsion; instead he had withdrawn from school, taking with him ninety-two others—"he goat men," according to Beecher, "butting everything in the line of their march which does not fall or get out of their way"—and reducing the enrollment of Lane Seminary from an even one hundred students to seven.[7]

Weld's tract, *American Slavery As It Is* (1839), one of the best known propaganda books for abolition, is an accumulation of newspaper clippings with appropriate comments.[8] The stories were, many of them, just the ones that Mrs. Stowe had heard from his own lips during Weld's Lane Seminary days. In her preface to the 1878 *Uncle Tom's Cabin* she acknowledged her use of the book and privately, to Weld's wife, Angelina Grimke, she went handsomely beyond her public testimony in her description of how "she kept that book in her work basket by day, and slept with it under her pillow by night, till its facts crystallized into Uncle Tom."[9]

Aside from such recognized obligations to Weld, Henson, and a few other agitators, Mrs. Stowe's story shares obvious similarities with other abolitionist and plantation fiction. Although Mrs. Stowe nowhere in her published writings admitted acquaintance with earlier antislavery novels, the situations and characters of both *Uncle Tom's Cabin* and *Dred* are partly traditional. In Richard Hildreth's *The Slave: or Memoirs of Archy Moore* (1836), the best written example of the type, the cruel overseer is a Yankee like Legree; Archy himself has the same combination of pride and sensitive feelings as George Harris, Eliza's husband; an easy-going squire with eighteenth-century liberal ideas is a possible, but not realized, St. Clare; and his son is the exact double of Tom Gordon in *Dred*, "a tyrant from whose soul custom had long since obliterated what little humanity nature had bestowed upon him."

Mrs. Stowe probably never saw *The Slave*, but the possibilities of borrowing details from earlier writers were almost limitless. A typical story that, with her fondness for Maria Edgeworth, the girl Harriet might well have read is one called "The Grateful Negro." In it were presented the differences between the good and the bad owner; the resulting contrast between the benevolent and the brutalized slave; the separation of families; and armed revolt, ending in martyrdom of the hero. The story is mild enough, but the picturesque details are such as might lie, almost forgotten, in the back of a child's mind.

Of all the sources of *Uncle Tom's Cabin*, the most decisive is the one least considered: the periodical for which it was written, whose policies were implicit in the shaping of the story. Here, as always, Mrs. Stowe was writing for an editor and a public whose expectations she could not afford to disregard. More than the author knew, her story was nourished, during its long period of serial publication, on the spirit of the *National Era* itself.

The *National Era* first appeared on January 7, 1847, with Gamaliel Bailey as editor and John Greenleaf Whittier as one of the associates. Its last issue was that of March 22, 1860, shortly after Bailey's sudden death. Mrs. Stowe had first known Bailey in Cincinnati where he had been a prominent citizen, a lecturer at Lane Seminary, and as early as 1836 a minor victim of riots deplored by Mrs. Stowe and by Henry Ward Beecher in the *Journal*. His *National Era*, which was a four-page weekly like the *Evangelist*, was issued in Washington, D. C., a more effective base of operation for abolitionists than the border city of Cincinnati.

From the start the *Era* expressed determined antislavery principles, but it was not exclusively a propaganda sheet. It reported congressional debates from its first issue, and it soon printed an appeal for the Irish poor, several articles favoring temperance, full accounts of the French revolution of 1848, and a news story on the woman's rights convention of the same year. Farther removed from such reforming activities, it ran an enthusiastic account of Jenny Lind, written by Fredrika Bremer, as well as an editorial on the same vocal artist; and reviews of books and magazines were a regular department.

The *Era* used a good proportion of literary material, poems and tales of unequal merit. Some were reprinted from Mrs. Sigourney, the New York *Evangelist*, Herman Melville, Lowell, and other sources; and supplementing these reprints were original contributions by T. S. Arthur, Mrs. Sigourney, Lucy Larcom, Grace Greenwood, Hawthorne, Bryant, and many others. Whittier himself supplied much verse and prose on such diverse subjects as Richard Baxter, Samuel Hopkins (the hero of *The Minister's Wooing*), and Lord Byron along with his routine journalistic editorials on the progress of the cause.

On the whole, the magazine justified its stated aim: "to mingle literature with politics . . . and to keep both subordinate to the great movement on behalf of human liberty." It was easy to read and no doubt effective. When Garrison's *Liberator,* a paper as much narrower than Bailey's *Era* as it was more evangelical, denounced it as "milk and water," the editor replied that "we take our stand as far South as we can" and "appeal to the Southern people as men of like passions with ourselves."[10]

Though the *Era* was conciliatory in intent, it occasionally described such horrors as the lashing and torturing of a colored maid mistakenly suspected of stealing from her owner (September 2, 1847). Her last words, however, were the meat of the account: "Let me say my prayers before I die." In this item, as throughout the magazine, the appeal was fundamentally moral. Many stories by Mrs. E. D. E. N. Southworth were used, with the editorial recommendation, "We need not say with what effect Mrs. Southworth uses fiction as a vehicle of truth."

Mrs. Southworth's serials, such as *Pride* and *Retribution,* were not abolitionist, for it was Bailey's policy to provide "original sketches and tales for home reading" along with political agitation. This was the need that Mrs. Stowe, as a young expert in the domestic and the moral, was also expected to serve. Of her four contributions before *Uncle Tom's Cabin,* only one mentioned the slavery issue. The first token of her antislavery sympathies was "The Freeman's Dream: A Parable," and it re-stated the editor's own view that the laws of God were above the Constitution of the United States. After this goodwill offering, she sent "A Scholar's Adventures in the Country," a mild satire against the impractical man; "Christmas, or the Good Fairy"; and "Independence," a story directed against late parties. All of these—printed between August 1, 1850, and January 30, 1851—were the type of mild sketch she had been doing for years; only on June 5, 1851, did her serial begin, preceded by an editorial announcement of May 8, 1851.

What had occurred in the meantime to distract her attention from late parties or impractical philologists like Calvin Stowe was, of course, the Fugitive Slave Act.[11] The *National Era* itself was full of stories and editorials denouncing it as early as September 26, 1850. In the issue of December 26, the first page of the paper contained her story "Christmas" and a discussion of the Act in Congress. On January 2, 1851, Whittier wrote against it. On June 5, it was discussed on the same page with the first installment of *Uncle Tom's Cabin*; and after that date, as before, it was a burning issue with both editors and contributors, who feared it as much as they hated it. These were the days in which even a small boy like Henry James observed that "the question of what persons of colour might or mightn't do was intensely in the air;"[12] and, along with the hot-house atmosphere of Mrs. Stowe's excited writing on the serial, the weekly fuel supplied by the *Era* contributed more than a mite to the increased emotion of later installments.

Uncle Tom's Cabin, or the Man that was a Thing, to use the original subtitle, began on June 5, 1851, and was concluded on April 1, 1852. During this entire period, Mrs. Stowe missed only two installments, a good record for the *National Era*. By October 30, 1851, the fan mail began with a letter making suggestions about future book publication. Shortly afterward the editor stated that "nearly all our readers" were showing great interest in the tale—this was directly after the death of Eva, which had been spread over four installments from November 20 to December 11, 1851. Book publication was announced on March 25, 1852; by the next week, when the final chapter appeared in the *National Era*, literary history was being made on a wider scale.[13]

After *Uncle Tom's Cabin* Mrs. Stowe's relationship with the *National Era* was not close. She sent in a few short original pieces, including a moral tale, "Don't You Like Flowers?", an article on temperance in Maine, and a plea to the Presbyterian Church to take a strong antislavery stand. Her further association was mostly through reprints and the magazine's comments on the triumphal progress of *Uncle Tom's Cabin*. For an entire year the paper was filled with praises of her and with replies to her detractors.[14]

Mrs. Stowe reaped incalculable advantage from her contract with the *National Era*. It was as essential to her as the Fugitive Slave Act itself. Left to a normal development, a mild interest in freedom for the blacks could have produced only further water and milk sketches like "Immediate Emancipation" or "The Freeman's Dream." On the other hand, absolute frenzy over abolition would have got nowhere with *Godey's Lady's Book* or the other carefully noncommittal magazines of her apprenticeship. The *National Era* was the ideal encouragement to her expanded efforts; it never shocked her as the *Liberator* did, and it exerted steady pressure towards writing about freedom. Not only did it furnish her with a commercial outlet, without which she never wrote; more important, it fed her with indignation and fury and, on occasion, with details for the advancement of her story. Its absorption in the wrongs of the colored race was a tremendous help to her: by taking her mind from petty domestic problems, it allowed her sense of her own servitude to identify itself with the most widely appealing issue of the day. The added circumstance that the *Era* had no standard of literary style to embarrass her into attitudinizing was not the least of its services to her, for it allowed her to write freely for a specific public of sympathetic souls.

CHAPTER *4*

The Years Between

FOLLOWING the sensational success of her first novel, Mrs. Stowe had the clear duty of maintaining her reputation. This led to other books on slavery until the Civil War, the Emancipation Proclamation, and Lee's surrender at Appomattox closed the account. Success made Mrs. Stowe a celebrity, justified her life, and offered her the next stage of a career. For the moment it also created the problem of facing public criticism. Typified by the objections of the London *Times,* a particular irritant to the Stowes, opposition to *Uncle Tom's Cabin* was strongly stated from the beginning by abolitionists, supporters of slavery, lovers of art, and mere perverse objectors to best-sellers.[1]

I *Some Attacks on* Uncle Tom's Cabin

Without attempting an exhaustive study of this contemporary adverse criticism, one can soon discover three sources from which it proceeded. First, and fewest, were critics who cavilled at such artistic deficiencies as faulty characterization, passages in bad rhetorical taste, and lapses from standard English usage. Second, and most numerous, were advocates of either slavery or abolition who complained about factual errors in the book. Third, and by all odds the most annoying to the author, were critical souls who cast reflections upon her motives, who attempted to disentangle the psychological riddle of her personality or to formulate rationally her unexpressed presuppositions about human nature.

Adverse comment of these first two types needs no elaborate marshalling of evidence here. In reviewing the third type of adverse comment, a distinction must be made between justified speculation and inexcusable scurrility. When the South Carolina poet William J. Grayson denounces Mrs. Stowe, there is more than a question of propriety in lines like these:

> A moral scavenger, with greedy eye. . . .
> On fields where vice eludes the light of day,
> She hunts up crimes as beagles hunt their prey;
> Gleans every dirty nook—the felon's jail
> And hangman's mem'ry, for detraction's tale,
> Snuffs up pollution with a pious air,
> .Collects a rumor here, a slander there;
> With hatred's ardor gathers Newgate spoils,
> And trades for gold the garbage of her toils.[2]

Mrs. Stowe suffered more violent abuse than this. According to the *National Era* of May 12, 1853, Richmond papers described her as a coarse, ugly, ill-natured, ill-mannered old woman; the New York *National Democrat* called her a hypocrite because she had declined to contribute to a cause which it knew was worthy; Bennett's New York *Herald* lampooned her violently; and many papers denounced her as a libeller of her country and as a sycophantic ally of the British redcoats. More of the same sort of abuse was so common and, as Mrs. Stowe knew, so unjustified that it was inevitable she should rise in heated defense of her personality and motives.

Of all such personal attacks, one of the most delightful, as well as the most inept, was that of an anonymous and poetical "Lady in New-York," *The Patent Key to Uncle Tom's Cabin; or, Mrs. Stowe in England,* printed at New York in 1853.[3] This extraordinarily bad poem, inspired by Mrs. Stowe's two books and her trip to Europe, but especially by *Uncle Tom's Cabin,* is a taxidermist's delight. It tempts quotation since, in addition to displaying a charming lack of rhyming ability, it combines practically all of the respectable prejudices against Mrs. Stowe:

> While some will find, in "Uncle Tom",
> A subject good to build upon;
> But show an "Uncle Tom", and then,
> I will believe that one has been;
> A case like "Uncle Tom's"—might be—

But when a thing like that I see,
Or appertaining thereunto,
Then I'll believe as many do,
That owning and protecting slave
Is greatest sin this side of grave.

That the Lady was grimly determined never to be forced to any such admission is clear from a later quatrain:

If *subject*—"Uncle Tom" I mean—
They think a great and mighty theme—
Just stay at home—our land's bereft!
There's not an "Uncle Tom" here left!

(Chivalry requires the admission that the italics and all marks of punctuation in the quoted passages are the Lady's.)

Having thus disclosed Mrs. Stowe's utter ignorance of the Southern slaves, the rhyming Lady proceeded to the minor suspicions forced upon her by *Uncle Tom's Cabin.* She considered it sacrilege in a New Englander to question a classification of humanity instituted by the Almighty Father. She questioned the patriotism of a woman who could attack the institutions of her native land but felt free to hobnob with foreigners. She went so far as to suspect, in italics, a mercenary purpose. Finally, the Lady was aware of basic impropriety in a woman's speaking out so boldly in public, no longer, as she should be, the tender vine clinging tremblingly to the sturdy oak for support.

In spite of the ineptitude with which it was phrased, the problem of Mrs. Stowe's personality stated in the anonymous Lady's *Patent Key* was real. Even so, the data of the problem need more careful consideration than she gave them. Instead of any imputation of dishonesty or knavish deception, one can accuse Mrs. Stowe of no greater error than faulty judgment: oblivious to the source or scope of her hysterical hatred of tyranny, she tried to save the world before learning to save herself.

An unseemly self-assurance, shown repeatedly in *Uncle Tom's Cabin,* is evinced with special clarity in the account of Eliza's refuge with Senator (a state senator, by the way) and Mrs. Bird, one of her first adventures after her successful escape across the Ohio River. The senator, to the disgust of his midget wife, an emotional dynamo and Noble Woman, had recently committed himself in favor of the Fugitive Slave Act; and the contrast between husband and wife reveals Mrs. Stowe's thoughts about the relative merits of man and woman. Her description of Mrs. Bird reads like an unconscious self-portrait:

> There are in this world blessed souls, whose sorrows all spring up into joy for others; whose earthly hopes, laid in the grave with many tears, are the seed from which spring healing flowers and balm for the desolate and distressed. Among such was the delicate woman who sits there by the lamp, dropping slow tears, while she prepared the memorials of her own lost one for the outcast wanderer (UTC, 164).

What deeds these little women can accomplish in the world! The result in this instance was that the senator, rising to his wife's moral code, broke the very law he had helped pass. Had not his wife revealed the higher justice? "It's a shameful, wicked, abominable law, and I'll break it, for one, the first time I get a chance" (97). There is perhaps not perfect consistency between this vigorous anarchistic nullification and her confidence that "everything will be set right,—if not in this life in another," or in her faith that "One who is not deaf, though he be long silent," will set affairs to right (138, 148). Devoted as she was, abstractly, to praise of Mother, Home, and Heaven, when she came concretely to observe the world about her, she saw it with jaundiced eyes.

In the last paragraph of her novel she further isolated herself from potential friends by openly attacking the Christian churches for "making a common capital of sin" by tolerating and protecting slavery. This final outburst was a call to battle, not the old Calvinistic battle between the churches and the Devil, but a new one of Mrs. Stowe against both churches and Devil.[4]

With her high motives publicly questioned by unsympathetic critics, a personal controversy was upon her to which she responded in what many of her friends considered the unwise *Key to Uncle Tom's Cabin*. Starting as a twenty-five page appendix to the novel, this argument in her own defense grew before publication into an entire volume. Unwise the book

may have been, to those who consider only chattel slavery;
Mrs. Stowe was not fighting for the Negro, however, but for
her ego.

II A Key to Uncle Tom's Cabin (1853)

In this sizeable volume—the fulfillment of a promise to present the "original facts and documents" upon which Mrs.
Stowe's novel was based—what was immediately apparent to
friends and foes alike was the paucity of her original data.
One visit to Kentucky, a diligent perusal of the *National Era,*
a few propaganda tracts, accounts of her brother Edward's
experiences with Elijah P. Lovejoy at Alton, Illinois, and a
study of partisan and incomplete works on the laws governing
slavery—these were all she had known to build upon. As she
frankly explained, writing without expectation of the excited
debates her novel was to cause, she had relied upon secondary
sources, which had, according to their custom, been less adequate than they appeared.

Her surprise is clear in her record of reading in the New York
Courier and Enquirer an article showing that in Louisiana,
where Tom was supposed to have been whipped to death and
a young slave girl publicly sold from her mother, both incidents
could never have occurred openly; they were acts which the
laws of the state declared criminal and punished as such. The
writer of this article took issue with another point dear to Mrs.
Stowe's heart by proving that the privation of religious instruction as she had described it, was "utterly unfounded in fact," and
by citing the first African churches of Louisville and Augusta,
with memberships of 1,500 and 1,300 respectively, as specimens
of churches entirely of, by, and for the slaves.

Though Mrs. Stowe might protest against this author's
personal judgments—"a ridiculously extravagant spirit of generalization pervades this fiction from beginning to end"—she
could not fail to realize the gaps in her information which his
article revealed (*Key,* 68). Answer him directly she could not,
for the facts were his; reply to him she could, for her cor-
roborative evidence—supplied by hundreds of correspondents
and found in Southern newspaper advertisements—revealed
to her the horror of the dispersion of black families and the
human tragedy of black slavery as she had only guessed them.

Knowing the humiliation of absolute subservience from her own childhood, she was on her true ground when she wrote, echoing Theodore Weld's ringing challenge, that "the deadly sin of slavery is its denial of humanity to man" (*Key*, 125). From this point of view, she could continue the argument begun in her novel: if the Negro is a man, what possible excuse can there be for denying him liberty and equality?

Righteous indignation, though an impressive weapon in controversy, led her away from her professed subject, Negro slavery. She threw about accusations and sarcastic remarks with a generosity that aroused opposition to even her soundest arguments. The last quarter of the *Key* renews the attack upon all the churches of America, the Quakers excepted, for their noncommittal or frankly favorable attitude towards slavery; and it was quite natural that, regarding the churches as the only means of securing abolition, she should have felt profoundly unhappy as she forecast the future. Nonetheless, to her opponents her comments appeared mere petulance in the face of biblical sanctions of slavery. In admitting that the Apostles had not been concerned with abolition, she gave the impression, as she frequently did throughout her future life, of molding her Christianity to fit her private desires, then of accusing everyone but herself of being out of step.

III Dred (1856)

If the writing of *Uncle Tom's Cabin* was like an unavoidable explosion and the writing of *A Key to Uncle Tom's Cabin* like an unavoidable argument, the next book in the series, *Dred: A Tale of the Great Dismal Swamp*, took form as an unavoidable literary obligation. A second antislavery novel was obviously Mrs. Stowe's duty to her public and her publishers. Though she had no hope of immediate emancipation for the slaves, she did her duty conscientiously. "Her whole mind was wrought up in the story," she told one of her publishers, "and she would pace the floor late at night dictating to her amanuensis."[5] Though freedom might be farther away than ever, after the subsiding enthusiasm of the fugitive slave days there was still opportunity for antislavery fiction.[6]

To the author, the initial reception of *Dred* was more than satisfactory. After four years of the golden publicity of controversy, the new novel was off to a better early sale than its predecessor. Soon Mrs. Stowe was able to ask significantly, as the royalties began to pour in, "After that who cares what critics say?" (AF, 222).

The question might still be asked, now that time has thrust *Dred* into the stacks of forgotten novels from which *Uncle Tom's Cabin* has been miraculously separated. Stylistically no better than the other, *Dred* lacked the essential breath of life. It was too largely what it purported to be, a book about the black slaves, a much less inspiring subject to Mrs. Stowe than the little wisp of a New England woman whose cause she had championed so ardently in her first novel. In an aesthetic valuation, forty years of suffering were worth more to Mrs. Stowe than the two years of writing that went into *Dred*.[7]

Even in the narrower sense of literary craftsmanship, the comparative failure of *Dred* can be understood. For one reason, the different kinds of material in the book were poorly pieced together. In spite of the documentary evidence submitted in the appendix, romantic paraphernalia was used unabashedly; and Dred himself, the prophetic leader of his race, was, except for the detail of pigmentation, a hero from Scottish history, a wild chieftain fleeing for safety to an inaccessible stronghold from which he sallied forth to confound the oppressors of his people. His conversation, a mélange of biblical passages, was a continuous, intense declamation; and at the sound of his voice, invisibly carried through the night air, even the heartless slave-owning class trembled, self-conscious of its sin.

For a time, as the story developed, hints were offered that Mrs. Stowe would counsel the slaves to arise and slay the tyrants—as John Brown was later to attempt and as Professor Stowe had once urged in a moment of excitement—but timely reflection led her to an alternative solution: a saintly death for her hero. His dying, as noble as his living, suggested the inadequacy of force in solving a problem that she continued to regard as primarily religious.

Around an utterly fantastic core of swamp-girdled retreats and mysterious, handy sorties, she conducted a more realistic discussion of the subject that was still among her main interests: "the degenerate Christianity of the slave states" (II, 22). She constantly wondered at the loyalty of the Southern clergy to their own social institutions. They must be fools, or knaves, she was sure; and through her pages she conducted a veritable parade of reverend gentlemen defending slavery or protesting that nothing could be done to abolish it. The nonconformist Dickson, single exception to the worldliness and wickedness of his brethren, was rewarded for his outspokenness with insults and violence. Naturally enough, the Northern clergymen were also taken to task; for they were still, in spite of her *Key*, out of step with Mrs. Stowe.

Accompanying these discussions of the religious situation, Mrs. Stowe attempted a complete survey of the economic life of the South. As she had never been in the Carolinas, the scene of her story, she was compelled to depend upon items in the *National Era*—most of which originated in Virginia; republished court records; and information volunteered by others sharing her views. Despite such difficulties, she succeeded in introducing a wide variety of recognizable types: the prosperous, kindly plantation owner; the poorer owner, more kindly still, forced by necessity to dispose of his human property; the vicious, drunken, lustful debauchee to whom she was pleased to refer as the flower of Southern chivalry, "adept in every low form of vice" (I, 46); the poor white, a coarse creature debased by competition with unpaid labor. Conventional though these characters were, the whites in *Dred* exhibited more diversity than the blacks; for the former had the choice of being good or bad, while the latter had apparently all been created good, predestination arranging only a difference in suffering. This sociological romancing, along with the theological tracting, was strung upon the unsubstantial cord of a love story.

In Mrs. Stowe's philosophy of fiction a novel meant a few pages of such startling action as lynchings and cholera epidemics sandwiched between generous portions of unprogressing discussion. Such spasmodic action in *Dred* was less successfully managed than in *Uncle Tom's Cabin* because of its triviality in comparison with the great causes associated with it. The love affair between a "princess of little flirts," Nina Gordon, and the idealistic master of four hundred slaves, Edward Clayton, meant so little to the author herself that she disposed of the heroine two hundred pages from the end of the story, so that the hero would be free to devote his undivided attention to his colored brethren. Nina Gordon's beautiful death might have appealed more strongly to the emotions if little Eva had not died so much more appealingly and if poor Sue Cripps, wife of a brutal poor white, had not, in this very book, preceded her into the Great Beyond.

Throughout *Dred* the hard-pressed author overworked her memories of *Uncle Tom's Cabin*. Thus Old Tiff, or Uncle Tiff, is another Uncle Tom; and Harry, a superior young slave, is Eliza's husband almost to a tittle. The old ideas also reappear; for Mrs. Stowe was never to cease believing that Negroes, half-blacks included, could easily pass for white in the South and that young Southern white men were physical weaklings.

Ineptly as some of the details of the story were arranged, *Dred* showed Mrs. Stowe's melancholy courage in facing the discouraging task of abolition. Between the indifference of the North and the entrenchment of the South, she saw no hope for emancipation; the efforts of a few individuals counted for nothing against the opposition of the organized churches and states. Realizing the impossibility of her own ideal of the gradual education of the slaves to prepare them for the responsibilities of freedom, she could only recommend that they flee from their bondage to the North or, preferably, to Canada or to Liberia, where they could add the joy of freedom to the consolations of Christianity. It is remarkable that of all the gifts she wanted for the Negroes—the social and moral virtues of the New Englanders (plus jolly dancing)—the one that they would first receive, legal emancipation, was that which she least anticipated.

IV *Sunny Memories of Foreign Lands (1854)*

Success never spoiled Mrs. Stowe. Criticism or opposition irritated her; but, once it was overcome, she regained her sweet composure and her kindly solicitude for all mankind. To soften the furious controversies of the 1850's, she sought relaxation in European travel. The first of her three trips was so memorable that she perpetuated her feelings and thoughts in a two-volume work, *Sunny Memories of Foreign Lands* (1854), which consisted of her letters home, a preface by her husband, and several chapters supplied by her brother Charles, another member of her party.

From one point of view, it was not much of a trip—the standard grand tour of Great Britain, France, Germany, Switzerland and Belgium—but the respect and adoration of those who met her gave her more pleasure than she had known. Guidebook in hand, following Walter Scott through Scotland and Martin Luther through Germany, she enjoyed even the conventional round of inspection; and between the visits to cathedrals and ragged schools there were stupendous gatherings in her honor.

Wherever she went, in Great Britain particularly, celebrities assembled at the dinners and receptions held for her. Macaulay, Gladstone, Dickens, Sir William Hamilton, Lady Byron, and Mrs. Jameson were a few of those she met and commented upon freely in her letters. Greatly as the literary men aroused her curiosity and much as the sturdy peasants and the honest Liverpool laborers pleased her with their Christian character, she found her greatest delight in meeting the aristocracy. With gusto she entered into her letters the splendid titles of duke and duchess, lord and lady, marquis and marchioness. With some of them, she exhibited a good deal of interest in reform movements, such as prohibition for Scotland; but one of her greatest delights was a concert concerning which she wrote to her husband, "Well, the Hons. and Right Hons. all were there. I sat by Lord Carlisle."

After leaving England, she was given more opportunity to rest and to recover the strength sapped out of her by her hospitable British hosts. She was rather critical of what she found on the mainland, sunny as her memories were. She was dissatisfied with the collection at the Louvre, looking in vain for pictures "great and glorious enough to seize and control my whole being." Catholic cathedrals distressed her Christian soul with their "horrible and loathesome idolatry" and their poor worshippers "kneeling with clasped hands and bowed heads, praying with an earnestness which was sorrowful to see." Even the Swiss Alps threatened to fail her, because so many of them were simply stones, until she found Mt. Blanc; and patriotism led her to prefer Niagara to it.[8]

In this exacting mood she rode about the Continent, meditating on philanthropy and Calvinism, eagerly comparing her impressions of the galleries with the dicta in her guidebooks, and writing prodigious letters chronicling the adventures of her inner and outer lives.

No wonder she had a good time. She brought home not only sunny memories, but keepsakes too: pebbles from the Tweed, testimonials from co-workers, and a volume of sermons given her by the Archbishop of Canterbury, "relating to the elevation and christianization of the masses." More precious than these knick-knacks, she brought a new tolerance for others; a special love for England, " kind-strong old England—the Mother of us All"; and a realization that the French were not incapable of religious feeling. Worried as she was by her admiration for chivalry and feudalism as perhaps inconsistent with the spirit of Christ, she had been so often thrilled by beauty that criticism of the Puritans as lacking in aesthetic appreciation took on a new, stronger meaning.

Mrs. Stowe's second visit to Europe in 1856, though equally successful, was more pleasant because less formal and exhausting than her first grand tour. With her pleasure trip she combined the satisfying business of securing a British copyright for *Dred*; and the enormous initial sale of the book, in England as in America, she interpreted as a token of the favor of God, who was bestowing upon her more of this world's goods than she had dared ask in her prayers. For her regular journalistic work, she sent public letters, personal and lively like *Sunny Memories,* to her magazine, the *Independent.*

With her international royalties safe and her reputation in the ascendant, she light-heartedly renewed old acquaintances among the aristocracy and formed new attachments. From the Duchess of Sutherland she received gratifying news: the Queen herself was eagerly reading *Dred,* which, as later communications revealed, she ranked above *Uncle Tom's Cabin.* It was on this trip that Mrs. Stowe enjoyed three happy days at the home of Charles Kingsley, whose novels of social protest she admired, and was astonished to learn that the literary divine was a zealous Anglican. When she visited Ruskin, it was the Englishman's turn to be astonished, in the first place, because she preferred "going in a boat on the river" to examining the notable manuscripts at Durham and, in the second place, because there was no river fit for boating, but only a trickle about as big as "a not very large town drain."⁹

There were no major literary results of this second European jaunt, but upon her third and last visit abroad (1859) during the final happy stage passed in Italy, she not only sent lengthy dispatches to the *Independent* but also began a historical novel, *Agnes of Sorrento.* These were indeed happy days, during which she lived gloriously on the success of *Uncle Tom's Cabin* and *Dred.* Of her new friends, the most important to her was Mrs. Fields, wife of the Boston publisher and later her capable biographer.

During these active, productive years, when her moral indignation was riding high, the only personal sorrow to disturb her sense of wholesome achievement was the death in 1857 of her eldest son, Henry. The boy, a freshman at Dartmouth College, died suddenly of drowning, and to her natural bereavement was added the ancient fear of damnation; for Henry had not been formally saved. "I may not be what the world calls a Christian," he had written, "but I will live such a life as every true man ought to live" (AF, 240). Alas! might his virtuous behavior be perhaps not enough? Was not his death similar to Professor Fisher's about which Catherine had never reassured herself completely? Might he not, as her father had taught, be damned?

Through this crisis of doubt Mrs. Stowe reverted amazingly to girlhood fears heretofore banished by success. She composed a complete account of her affliction for the Duchess of Sutherland and another for her daughters in Paris. To her sister Catherine she confessed that the old temptations of the Devil assailed her; and her soul hung in the balance as she feared that her trust in God had been misplaced. When at length she recovered her faith in Jesus, she was greatly pleased by her husband's visions, in which Henry's presence returned accompanied by the vibration of a mysterious guitar. More comforting still was the final explanation, agreed upon between them, that the guitar, since Henry was no musician, must have been struck by Eliza, the Professor's first wife (AF, 153; CES, 350).

The direct literary results of the vacation travels of these middle years, the book *Sunny Memories* and her public correspondence, are revelatory rather than intrinsically valuable. Her double handicap as a traveler was inexperience and a lack of caution. In too many ways she was so embarrassingly American.

V   *Men of Our Times (1868)*

Aside from her writing, Mrs. Stowe's personal contributions to winning the Civil War were minimal. As a woman of fifty, unless she had volunteered as a nurse, active service could hardly have been expected of her. "All that women can do," she had said during the Kansas trouble "is to keep their husbands awake nights, with their sighing and groaning."[10] In the big war, as in the little one that had preceded it, hers was the woman's part of sighing and groaning and responding to patriotic hysteria.

Mrs. Stowe's cooperation in the war was indirect. Her second son Frederick William was among the earliest volunteers, and his services, including promotion in rank and serious injury at Gettysburg, offered the glamor of storybook heroism as well as an opportunity for personal intercession on his behalf with military and political authorities. The solemnity of the great public gatherings thrilled her, and like other people she was "inspirited" by the military music "in which the soldiers joined with hearty voices" (AF, 260). She responded wholeheartedly to the appeal of cheering people, of waving handkerchiefs, of fine-looking army chaplains, and especially to the delirium of a religious festival in the capital city at which a thousand redeemed slaves prayed and sang hymns.

Such excitement was in itself almost too strenuous for her, but it was pleasant, whereas her private life, continuing in the habitual flurry of nervousness, was filled with trouble. Existence was further complicated by several changes in residence, first from Andover to Hartford, Connecticut, when her husband retired from teaching, and later within the city of Hartford, when after two years the house built to her bizarre specifications was abandoned because of the intrusion of industry into the neighborhood. The wedding of her daughter reduced her, as she phrased it, to "sheer imbecility"; and other domestic exigencies kept her continually worried and discontented.

She found, nevertheless, much to arouse that sense of moral indignation which she esteemed a chief among the virtues. From time to time arose such crises as the impudent question asked by the Congregationalist ministers of England as to why the North did not let the South go. And there were always, in otherwise dull moments, the "Horrible barbarities" of the Southern soldiers. As her specific war services she wrote essays for the *Independent* and the *Atlantic Monthly* on the prosecution of the campaign, patriotic poems about the war to end war, as well as an important "Appeal to the Women of England," in reply to an address she had received from them some eight years previously.[11] Amid the desolate hearths and ruined homesteads of which she spoke, she was sustained by the knowledge that she was assisting at "the throes and ravings of the exorcism" of slavery, and the conclusion of the war left her spiritually satisfied if physically depleted. As though to emphasize the final ascendency of the North, she moved, as soon as was practical— that is, in 1868—to Florida, where she could examine firsthand the work of reconstruction and firmly guide the freedmen towards New England virtue.

Upon one principle she finally agreed with Garrison, who had declared in closing the books of the Anti-Slavery Society, that slavery was ended. The Emancipation Proclamation fully satisfied her moral sense, and she was willing to allow as long a time as necessary for the full absorption of the Negro into political life. She looked forward calmly to an indefinite period during which brother Henry Ward and others of "moral influence" were to win over the "really good men" of the South. What to do with the former slaves in the new South was a problem she considered in articles for the *North American Review* and other magazines, but she realized that a solution was beyond her powers. Brooding over the situation, she could do nothing better in her book *Men of Our Times* than to fight again through the Civil War, still temperamentally in the midst of the combat.

Although she assembled it hastily from previous magazine articles and almost unwillingly except for the money it would bring, Mrs. Stowe thought well of this book. It would be good for young men and women to read, she was sure. She rather overemphasized it, however, for her eighteen biographical sketches are colorless and uninspiring.

Men of Our Times is a thoroughly provincial book. Mrs. Stowe was dreadfully in earnest in expounding the careers of the "leading patriots of the day," as the subtitle designated them: the statesmen, generals and orators whose high morality had demolished the "so-styled Southern aristocracy." These patriots included Lincoln; Grant; Garrison; Sumner; Chase; Henry Wilson, "the self-taught, fearless shoe-maker's apprentice of Natick" who became Governor of Massachusetts; Greeley; Farragut; John Andrew, "a consistently Christian State governor" of Connecticut; Colfax, speaker of the House; Stanton; Frederick Douglass, escaped slave and professional lecturer for the Anti-Slavery Society; generals Sheridan, Sherman, and Howard; William A. Buckingham, another governor of Connecticut; Wendell Phillips; and Henry Ward Beecher.

Of these sketches, only the last has intrinsic worth. Mrs. Stowe interpreted her brother with sisterly devotion, exulting in his every triumph, and sympathizing with such foibles as his abandonment of an interest in mathematics and the classics in favor of an abiding passion for phrenology. His opposition to tobacco and gin echoed her own. And she regarded his invention of a circular study table with a hole in the middle as an especially happy manifestation of a mind equipped to solve difficult problems.

After her brother, she particularly praised Grant, whose statesmanship impressed her as deeply as his military skill, and Sumner, the New England Brahmin whose advocacy of legal abolition contrasted favorably in her mind with the fanatical agitation of Garrison.

Naturally, all of the eighteen subjects of her sketches were praised, as they were the leading patriots of the day; but a clear difference distinguishes the adulation accorded some from the merely perfunctory approval of others. Abraham Lincoln, though honored in the opening and longest sketch, was not one of her favorites; and there was a scarcely concealed uneasiness in her troubled references to his "queer stories" and other traits incomprehensible to a New England lady.

Mrs. Stowe prided herself on her ability to dash off brief biographical sketches upon demand. One of her markets was a Baptist paper *The Watchman and Reflector,* for which a series on the patriots had been written. To make an impressive subscription volume, the shorter sketches were blown up against Mrs. Stowe's better judgment, and weakened appreciably. The life of Henry Ward Beecher, which was entirely new, had been wrung from her by means of an added thousand dollars. Next to the longest in the book, it is not only valuable documentarily but also as lively writing.

Insofar as *Men of Our Times* has a subject, it is the achievement of a Christian democracy. The rebellion, which she regarded as the fulfillment of biblical prophecy, was her villain. Recognizing that slavery was but one type of injustice, she occasionally reminded her readers of the dangers of drink, tobacco, and dancing. She did indeed show, as she had promised, the racial histories of her men (over half were New Englanders, over one-third were direct lineal descendants of the Puritans); but she badly neglected another aim as she would never have done a few years later—a consideration of the characters and influence of mothers—with Garrison alone rising to the full height of her opportunities. For the rest, the book is jumbled fact and fancy, rehashed anecdotes, and praise of the "untitled aristocracy of Boston."

With *Men of Our Times,* Mrs. Stowe bade farewell to the questions of slavery and rebellion that had inspired a series of books beginning with *Uncle Tom's Cabin.* One may grant that the enslavement of human beings is a sin and a crime which had needed to be proclaimed with vigor, even with excitement or hysterical emphasis. If such was the purpose for which life had prepared her, she had performed it, in some two thousand pages of print, with commendable completeness. Emancipation, which had vindicated her cause, had robbed her of her literary materials; and, since she had not the slightest idea of retiring from active public life, she was ready to turn with the times to other moods and other subjects.

CHAPTER 5

Mother, Home, and Household Sermons

THE LITERARY ACTIVITY of Mrs. Stowe's maturity was stupendous. For a money-making career she continued writing for magazines as a steady grind, with long and short stories and articles composed at breakneck speed. Within ten or eleven years after the publication of *Dred* in 1856, she wrote ten or eleven books, including three of her most substantial novels; and within the ten years preceding 1878 she published fourteen more books. Eventually then, at sixty-seven, she was forced to take the rest she had long needed, a rest that proved to be permanent retirement. Her public hated to see her go; and as late as 1883 the rumor was spread that she was planning another novel, to be called *Orange Blossoms,* a rumor which she denied definitely, almost brusquely.

During these last productive years she wrote on a miscellany of subjects, from Byron to the Bible, eighteenth-century New England to modern New York and Florida, in poems, stories, and essays for men, women, and children. Only by close examination can these writings be gathered into two groups, amorphous at best: one with a New England background; the other with domestic life in the postwar reconstruction period. The more important group, a continuation of the early local color sketches, includes primarily five books: *The Minister's Wooing, The Pearl of Orr's Island, Oldtown Folks, Sam Lawson's Oldtown Fireside Stories,* and *Poganuc People.* To these should be added, as pendants in contrast, *Agnes of Sorrento* and *Palmetto-Leaves,* both of which describe civilizations alien to that which, in spite of the sorrow she had suffered from it, held her greatest loyalty.

The second amorphous group, dealing with social life—a continuation of the early moral sketches—includes three volumes of essays beginning with *House and Home Papers;* the three remaining novels, beginning with *My Wife and I;* and the treatise *The American Woman's Home.* With them belong also two books on religion which are in effect studies in the practical applications of religion in reconstruction America. The book on Byron, because of the important influence of Byron upon Mrs. Stowe's entire life, deserves individual analysis. The children's stories, also unaccounted for in this twofold division, can be disregarded without serious consequences, except as they add a touch of fantasy not exhibited elsewhere in her works: for the most part they contain the same ideas as her books for adults, with much the same expression.

Her Americanism was absolute, with three centers of interest and concern: the late eighteenth and early nineteenth centuries in New England, the years of antislavery agitation, and the troubled postwar years of rampant commercialism. In her stories she earnestly rebelled against cherished institutions of each of these periods—against Calvinism, against chattel-slavery, and against business laissez-faire. Though the power of constructive planning was denied her, she possessed the spirit of revolt and the energy to fight tooth and nail against the enemies of her faith.

I *Religious Tracts*

With a father, a husband, and seven brothers in the ministry, a woman would think about religion, whatever she might say before her men folks. For Mrs. Stowe, to think was to speak out strong, bold and often. With her faith that all problems are religious, she never felt that, even in her fiction, talk about religion was a digression from the subject at hand. Similarly, when she wrote her two special religious treatises—*Woman in Sacred History* (1873) and *Footsteps of the Master* (1877)— she never felt that turning from God was a departure from her professed subject.[1]

Her faith in the Deity was, the evidence indicates, the most constant of her preoccupations. Her earliest triumph as a school-girl writer had been won with a composition entitled "Can the Immortality of the Soul be Proved by the Light of Nature?" Her answer, at the age of twelve, was a clear no: "Never till the blessed light of the Gospel dawned on the borders of the pit and the heralds of the Cross proclaimed Peace on earth and good will to men, was it that bewildered and misled man was enabled to trace his celestial origin and glorious destiny."[2] Holding undeviatingly to this childhood conviction, she devoted an appalling number of pages to puzzling over the precise attributes demanded of the finest type of God. Her religious thinking was her special pride; her reflections upon Godhood were both her greatest comfort and her firmest conviction that she had something new and valuable to say.

Granting that there was more of the conventional or traditional in her beliefs than she realized, one need not attempt to answer categorically the question, Was she a Puritan? By the nineteenth century, the Yankees having succeeded them, there were no true Puritans: but Lyman Beecher must have been as near an approach to the classic models as was humanly possible. Mrs. Stowe was not entirely true to type, for the great Puritans were intellectual and not sentimental about their religion. She knew all the arguments; but, like her most famous brother, she discarded them. From her Aunt Harriet Foote, a high-church Episcopalian, she had learned at an early age some of the distinctions which were to disturb her for many years. Eventually she broke with her father's Calvinistic church and became an Episcopalian.

At the age of twelve she could write learnedly on abstruse doctrines; and when not much older she could have easily explained the distinction between supralapsarian, sublapsarian, and infralapsarian—because she had determined to be none of them. She knew Puritanism, that is, thoroughly; and she rejected it determinedly, denouncing "metaphysical analysis" and searching the Scriptures for gloriously beautiful and indistinct images (RS, 230).

Yet for all this determination she remained basically as completely fundamentalist as her father and her husband; and her departure from them was mostly a bodily shrinking from logical consequences. No matter how old she might grow, she would remain in her soul the same sweet, old-fashioned girl who had lisped her baby acquiescence. Her views were so bound by eighteenth-century Calvinism that, labor as she would, she could never escape from her father's harsh, uncongenial conclusions.

For example, she believed implicitly in witchcraft, on precisely Cotton Mather's grounds. "A witch was the dark shadow of a prophetess," she wrote in *Woman in Sacred History*. "A prophetess was a holy woman drawing near to the spiritual world by means of faith and prayer, and thus inspired by God with knowledge beyond the ordinary powers of mortals." No doubt she numbered herself among the prophetesses, for each of them was a poetess like her, and they were uniformly "married women and mothers of families, and not like the vestal virgins of antiquity, set apart from the usual family duties of women." Since the prophetess must be accepted on unquestionable biblical authority, what pious Christian could doubt the Witch of Endor and the other wizards and witches of sacred history? "A witch, on the contrary," she explained, carrying on the contrast, "was one who sought knowledge of the future, not from the one supreme God, but through all those magical charms, incantations and ceremonies by which the spirits of the dead were sought for interference in the affairs of men" (WSH, 17, 93, 165).

This gentle deprecation of witchcraft is her rather mild substitute for Cotton Mather's multitude of vigorous, vicious devils. "The guilt and folly of seeking" these extra-biblical assurances, she continued directly, "consisted in the fact that there was another and a legitimate supply for that craving of the human heart" (WSH, 165). In thus charitably interpreting witchcraft as a pathetic mistake instead of as a vicious crime, she found exactly the idea she wanted to remind her of a serious problem, spiritualism, which by this time she had come to mistrust as offering the same delusions and dangers as witchcraft of old.

The virgin birth interested her profoundly, and she envied Mary for having produced a child without male sexual cooperation. Jesus was entirely Mary's own, she explained in *Footsteps of the Master*, and she enjoyed a monopoly over him that no other mother has ever had (RS, 31-32). Lacking mortal father, Jesus was absolutely his mother's boy. As He was the union of the feminine and the divine, He had an understanding of women that other men cannot approach; and moreover, He is understood better by women, pure women, than by crude masculine creatures: "We can see no image by which to represent the Master," she concluded her cogitations, "but one of those loving, saintly mothers, who in leading along their little flock, follow nearest in the footsteps of Jesus" (RS, 78).

In this mood of exaltation she could hardly avoid another idea pleasant to her self-esteem: that through progressive revelations Christian womanhood had, in the nineteenth century, reached an unparalleled height, attaining, as she wrote in *Woman in Sacred History,* "that pure ideal of a sacred woman springing from the bosom of the family, at once wife, mother, poetess, leader, inspirer, prophetess" (WSH, 28). And well it would be for the world, she could proceed, if this biblical model were honored more dutifully by wavering manhood.

The one serious question which arose to disturb this rosy view was Mary's modest retirement. "It is remarkable," said Mrs. Stowe, hinting that it was also deplorable, "that Mary was never in any one instance associated in public work with Jesus" (RS, 38). Thus she phrased one of the paradoxes of her own life: she, who professed to believe in woman's domestic sphere, had been forever sticking her fingers into public pie and poking her stub nose into public business. There was only one explanation: "The delicacy of woman may cause her to shrink from the bustle of public triumph, but when truth and holiness are brought to public scorn she is there to defend, to suffer, to die" (RS, 39).

Personal disclosures like these are the most important part of Mrs. Stowe's writings on religion, for they show the definitely personal motives that led to these lay sermons. Her religious experiences were a rich part of her life and deeply significant to her, but the only doctrine she could express was her absolute faith that Jesus saves those who love and serve him.

II *The Christian Home*

Mrs. Stowe never suspected, one may be sure, that a paradox of her simplified theology was her working hypothesis that heaven was of less importance to her than earth. Only worldlings can be as concerned with the need for money as she was. Her calm assurance of self-righteousness knew none of the doubts of Jonathan Edwards or Lyman Beecher. About human nature she was as skeptical as they, with the single exception that she made of herself. Always righteous if not always right, she was a Christian mother, an example to the land, and the world was her oyster.

What should have been a revelatory book was the direct outgrowth of this assurance. Its title, briefly rendered as *The American Woman's Home,* bore the following additional explanation: "Principles of Domestic Science; being a guide to the formation and maintenance of economical, healthful, beautiful, and Christian Homes." It was published under her name and Catherine's in 1869; but other work prevented her from contributing much beyond her name.

The American Woman's Home, since it is jointly attributed to Mrs. Stowe, no doubt has use as a commentary on her thought; but the expression, alas, is not her own, and much of it is merely a revision of Catherine's many-versioned treatise on domestic economy. The exposition of the Christian family, of scientific domestic ventilation, of healthful drinks, doubtless met with Harriet's thorough approval, and the chapter on the care of servants seems particularly in keeping with her ideas. Nevertheless, intrinsic delight notwithstanding, the pleasure of examining the work in detail must be foregone.

The omission is the less serious since both fiction and essays show her mature convictions on most of these subjects. From her serial novels and magazine articles may be retrieved in scattered comments the principles that might, under happier circumstances, have been organized into a major treatise. They will be found, virtually unaltered for tender intelligences, in stories for children, *Queer Little People* and *Little Pussy Willow,* reprinted from the magazine *Our Young Folks.*

For man and beast she invoked the same immutable morality. In the animal stories of *Queer Little People* (1867) virtue and vice remain human, whether in the homely sketches of family pets or in the allegories that comprise the two halves of the volume. The morals of the allegories are standard: don't steal, proved by the story of a squirrel; don't yield to evil temptations, proved by the story of a robin that fell from its nest; don't be a meddler, proved by the story of a magpie. A narrative involving Miss Katydid and Miss Cricket is supposed to show the folly of drawing a color line.

Little Pussy Willow (1870), a less harrowing Pollyanna, is an extended fable (123 pages) expounding the difference between the wholesome life of a country child and the pampered existence of a vain daughter of wealth. The philosophy of the story, which must have done a great deal of good to little girls, was variously stated: "It is not so much what people *have* that makes them happy, as what they think and feel about what they have" (p. 9); or, "Now the greatest trouble about girls and women is, not that they think too much of outside beauty, but that they do not think enough of inside beauty" (p. 62); or, "Now remember to be a good girl, and to help other people" (p. 123). Overflowing with such good counsel, Mrs. Stowe further enriched the narrative (which is rather lame) with descriptions of bread making, interior decorating, and healthful clothing. She could· appropriately have called her tale "The American Little Woman's Home."

For adult readers more advice was generously introduced into thicker volumes. *My Wife and I* (1871), the first of two social studies also including *We and Our Neighbors* (1875), was a novel closely adapted to the needs and tastes of subscribers to the *Christian Union,* in which both members of the sequence were serialized. More will be said later about this publication, but its general flavor can be inferred from the serials themselves.

Considering the amount and quality of the writing she had published up to this time, a reader finds the stylistic incompetence of *My Wife and I* surprising as well as painful. Mrs. Stowe hardly needed to write down to any audience, however pious and humble; but the brutal truth is that she thoroughly approved of what she was doing, convinced that it must benefit publisher J. B. Ford's moral clientele.[3] If this story were typical of literature in the America of 1871, no one could disagree with the thought of its opening sentence: "the world is returning to its second childhood."

Specifically, *My Wife and I* recounts the rise of the narrator, Harry Henderson, from poverty to affluence and happy mating with a daughter of wealth. The conscientious son of a New Hampshire minister, Harry, knowing he was unworthy of following his father's calling, devoted himself to serious journalism in New York, prospered, found his Eva Van Arsdel—a sweet wholesome girl in spite of her worldly family—and set up house-keeping.

It is odd how like an old lady this Harry Henderson is, odd how thoroughly his ideas are those of Mrs. H. B. Stowe. Don't smoke or drink, he warns his readers; don't take lightly the advice of elders; don't be worldly; don't marry for money; don't let college undermine Christianity; don't neglect studying the Bible; don't become an aesthete, a reader of Rossetti or Swinburne; don't be vain about clothing; don't take a fashionable honeymoon trip; don't live in a rented house. To these principal commandments, others are added, sometimes with painstakingly thorough development. Evidently the readers of the *Christian Union* or the young girls to whom the story was dedicated were in a parlous state of danger; but they undoubtedly could take advice.[4]

In brief, *My Wife and I* is a tract barely disguised as a serial story. An appeal for greater privileges for young women, it confuses that issue by its sarcastic portraits of two types of feminist leaders, Mrs. Cerulian (also spelled Cerulean) and Miss Audacia Dangyereyes (also spelled Dangereyes); both are based upon types recognized in the contemporary feminists, Mrs. Elizabeth Cady Stanton and Victoria Woodhull. To each, Mrs. Stowe does less than justice; she presents her Audacia as a shameless hussy and her Mrs. Cerulian as a dupe. Exactly what Mrs. Stowe desired for young women is difficult to determine; on the one hand, she wanted the world run by mothers; on the other, she didn't believe that women should have the vote.[5]

Her characters show the same confusion. The strong-minded girls have indistinct ambitions to do something with their lives, particularly to secure formal education, as in medicine, or to pursue other more vaguely described "professional studies." That is about as far as Mrs. Stowe's plans went. She was greatly worried about the world, which was not virtuous, into which these newly educated women would be projected; and she did not know whether the finer clay of woman would overcome evil or succumb to its insidious influence. Humanity needs, says Harry Henderson for her, a loving and redeeming power by which it can be led back to virtue; but, on the other hand, as his father-in-law points out, *good* women are not fit to govern the world because they do not, and should not, know the rottenness of life.

No actual villain sullies these pages, no sharper or grosser sinner than Audacia Dangereyes; but gloomy hints are cast about the utter worldliness and frivolity of all except the chosen few idealists. Rogues, sharpers, pickpockets, and bullies are so numerous that a woman's general rule of conduct must be to take for granted that every man one meets will cheat if he can. Most horrible of all evils is that dirty, polluted literature by means of which, as Harry Henderson agrees, "we are fast drifting to destruction, it is a solemn fact" (134).

In *We and Our Neighbors, or the Records of an Unfashionable Street* (1875), Mrs. Stowe fulfilled after four years a promise to continue the story of Harry and Eva Henderson's married life. So many loose ends were left dangling at the end of this second book that one judges the author had never fulfilled hopes of further extending the saga.

To the rules of conduct advanced in *My Wife and I* the sequel adds these: don't destroy faith in prayer; don't withdraw self-ishly from life; don't marry in haste; don't parody hymns or concoct puns out of Holy Writ; don't ignore bodily hygiene; don't nag the servants; and don't use Gothic type on Christmas cards.[6] Mrs. Stowe still believed that the function of women in social life was to ennoble men, and she propounded the physiological theory that girls were not so strongly tempted as men to depart from virtue, though she was well aware of the particular temptations inherent in dazzling feminine beauty. Distributed over 480 pages, there are enough rules of conduct to direct and enrich almost anybody's life; yet Mrs. Stowe's gloom persisted: "Don't it seem strange," said Eva to Harry, "how the minute one actually tries to do some real Christian work everything goes against one?" (257).

The story itself, designed to show how to be happy, shows more distinctly how easy it is to be unhappy. Marriage is its theme; and the one happy marriage in the book is that of Eva and Harry. In contrast, no fewer than six miserable women are paraded across the scene. These should be warnings enough against matrimony, but Mrs. Stowe blandly constructs her story around promoting marriages for two more of the Van Arsdel girls, Angelica and Alice.

In addition to the romantic, the other strain in this book concerns the entertainments given by Harry and Eva—jolly social gatherings in which ideas about religion are exchanged between the young men and women, neighbors on the street, and selected friends from the higher professions. Their conversations do not lead anywhere except to the altar, but they must have been reassuring to readers of the *Christian Union,* for they all go to show that "there never was a time faith in Christianity was so deep and all-pervading, and when it was working in so many minds as a disturbing force" (439).

To *We and Our Neighbors* has been reserved an honor rarely bestowed upon Mrs. Stowe's social novels, that of being reviewed at its appearance by a first-rate critic. Young Henry James, already embarked upon his career as literary craftsman, carefully examined the curious work. "It would be rather awkward to attempt to tell what Mrs. Stowe's novel is about," he confessed, mystified by its formlessness and vulgarity. The speech of the first families of New York, as he saw it reproduced by Mrs. Stowe, struck him as a combination of rural Yankee dialect, Negro jargon, and paragraphs from the *Home Journal.* "None of Mrs. Stowe's ladies and gentlemen open their mouths without uttering some amazing vulgarism," he continued, content to remark that in addition to Eva, with her interest in *the humanitarian questions of the day,* "There are a great many people, of whose identity we have no very confident impression, inasmuch as they never do anything but talk—and that chiefly about plumbing, carpetlaying, and other cognate topics" (New York *Nation,* XXI [1875], 61).

Of a piece with these two novels is yet a third effort to set the world to rights. Though identified on the title page as a society novel, *Pink and White Tyranny* (1871) is also described in the author's preface as "not to be a novel" but "a little commonplace history," "a story with a moral," a "sketch" and a "parable." The latter description is the true one; and the moral, told succinctly like the legend under a cartoon, is that no family should ever be led into divorce. "When once marriage is made and consummated, it should be as fixed a fact as the laws of nature" is one of the ways in which Mrs. Stowe phrases her proposition; and she includes even marriage to

such a "shopworn flirt" and "selfish, heartless little creature"
as Lillie Ellis.[7]

Pink and White Tyranny is partly a warning against hasty
marriages with strangers and partly a satire against the type of
woman Lillie was: a selfish flirt who liked French novels,
who smoked cigarettes and lacked religious sense, who wanted
to serve wine at the dinner table and had no motherly instinct.
But it was not Mrs. Stowe's custom to let her story decide its
own meaning. Having determined to attack divorce, she main-
tains that purpose, though the attack is by indirection and
likely to be entirely overlooked unless emphasized by special
notes.

Throughout *Pink and White Tyranny* she is worried by the
French influence on American life. When John Seymour finds
that his wife has been fibbing about her age, avowing only
twenty years instead of the true twenty-seven, Mrs. Stowe
remarks that "a Frenchman would have smiled in amusement
on the detection of the pretty feminine *ruse*," and that "only
an Englishman or an American can understand the dreadful
pain of that discovery to John" (95-96).

Poor little pink and white Lillie is on the whole a warning
against French frivolity rather than the more horrible vices.
"France, unfortunately, is becoming the great society-teacher
of the world," the author generalizes; and inasmuch as "the
Celtic races have a certain sympathy with deception," it is
easy enough to see that if no just, generous, manly, religious
young Anglo-Saxon fellow ever looked longingly upon such as
she, he would never be tempted to divorce her. The moral
ought to be that every "good solid chip of the old Anglo-Saxon
block" should avoid young ladies who possess "the doubtful
talent of reading French with facility" (93, 96, 107, 204).

III *Essays on Domestic Life*

If as a social novelist Mrs. Stowe was at her weakest, as a
social essayist the change was more in manner than in matter.
To express her ideas, which were on the whole more suitable
to essay than to story, she adopted for her *House and Home
Papers* (1865) a style well recognized as acceptable to the better
magazines in which more editorial attention was given to the

niceties of expression than in the churchly journal for which she contrived her fictional serials. Not so unforcedly cultured as that of George William Curtis or so frank as that of Ik. Marvel, her one-time editorial associate on *Hearth and Home*, her essay style emphasized the same vivacity of manner that had opened to these writers, among other markets, *Putnam's Magazine* and the *Southern Literary Messenger*.

A congenial opportunity was afforded her in the articles—period pieces from the *Atlantic Monthly*—which were collected as *House and Home Papers* (1865), *Little Foxes* (1866), and *The Chimney-Corner* (1868). The type was well understood, the narrow scope of its satire recognized, and its underlying sentimentalism assumed. As Christopher Crowfield, a tolerant, benevolent old body, she was given permission to write freely on the aspects of home-making she desired. Taking for her motto "No work of art can compare with a perfect home,"[8] she ranged far and wide, dispensing wisdom lavishly, restrained only, and perhaps aware of the check upon her, by the conventions of the type.

Remember the difference between a house and a home, she counseled her readers, anticipating the heap o' living hypothesis of a later authority. Don't try to have a stylish parlor, she warned them. The most beautiful furnishings are always the cheapest, she reminded them in one article, and was inspired to continue the subject in the following. She advised against a too-expensive carpet, since by spending less on the floor covering money might be saved for "engravings, chromolithographs, or photographs of some really *good* works of art."[9]

In the course of his monthly ramblings Christopher Crowfield frequently returned to the subjects nearest Mrs. Stowe's heart. On more than one occasion he came out unequivocally for woman suffrage—thus expressing one of her attitudes towards that puzzling proposal. He wrote caustically about French morals and manners; he showed a high regard for the manners and morals of New England. But among all the subjects connected with the home, his (or her, if you prefer) greatest attention—more than to religion, hygiene, entertainment, even furnishings—was centered on the servant problem, which was, as he described it, "woman's natural, God-given employment of *domestic service*."[10]

The manner of these homey, housey articles is relentlessly genial. Interspersed with references to Milton and Shakespeare, to Bacon, Pope, and Fénelon, to "old Plato" and "old Ben Jonson"—for Christopher was presumed to be a bookish man—they are dominated finally by familiar texts from "the dear old book of comfort." Their merit is a solid morality, for they are household sermons; and they must have pleased the author into thinking that they would do a great deal of good in reminding the dear *Atlantic* readers to avoid extravagance and folly in their homes.

If Mrs. Stowe had spoken frankly for herself without ringing in Crowfield like a ventriloquist's dummy, her essays might have possessed at least autobiographical value; but the reader must always struggle to remember that in these three books she never speaks directly in character. The disguise is transparent; yet obvious as it may be that Crowfield is not speaking—for the lady's desire to be a man could not endow her with masculinity—she may not be speaking either. More often than not, no one is speaking and no one is being addressed.

All of these didactic writings, the fiction no less than the Crowfield essays, are now peculiarly empty. Written for the magazines,[11] they were commercially valuable and kept money pouring into the family coffers, which were generally low in spite of publishers' advances and queenly fees. As books they were acceptable to the readers for whom they were intended, so that Mrs. Stowe could afford to overlook the carping criticism of such organs of opinion as the *Nation*—in which Henry James's review of *We and Our Neighbors* appeared—just as she had been able to overlook the more strenuous criticism of her earlier novels in the golden days before the war.

But the principal gain for her writing was that her examination of the troubled, unmalleable world in which she lived intensified her affection for the vanished New England of her early girlhood and her husband's memories. With the exhaustion of the present as material for her writing, her subject became more definitely limited to the one. in which her best qualities could be better displayed.

CHAPTER 6

God's Countries

I *New England*

IN THAT very provincial expression of opinion, the elementary textbook on geography on which she permitted her name to appear as author in 1855, Mrs. Stowe shows how completely New England was her center of the universe and test of moral excellence.[1] With the whole world to choose from, the first locality studied is New England; the first state mentioned, Connecticut; and the first college, Yale.

At the earliest opportunity, the story of the Pilgrims on the *Mayflower* is told, and the lesson to be drawn from it is repeated for the children of America:

> The descendants of the Pilgrim Fathers in New England have been distinguished for their reverence for the Bible, for their good schools, and for their industrious habits. This is the reason why no people in the world have been more prosperous in every kind of business than those in New England; for God always makes those most prosperous who are most obedient to his laws in the Bible (42).

The rest of the world has been created to set off New England's brilliance. Holland is a place "where the Pilgrim Fathers first went before they landed in New England"; the Quakers are admirable because they are "as careful as the New England people to have good schools"; and the Westerners of the frontier draw virtues, such as they have, from Puritan forebears.

If region can be bred in the bone, two hundred years of New England Beechers had bequeathed to Mrs. Stowe the spirit of that rocky, inhospitable shore. She had been brought up to have faith in New England, to see no virtues apart from it, and to regard it as the home of the latest chosen people. In family chronicles, in her father's gorgeously colorful recollections, and in her husband's Yankee anecdotes, she found not only background for fiction, but plots as well—and these served as restraining framework from which she could not stray as lamentably as in her attempts to intuit the psychology of New York's best people. She understood New Englanders better; and, like Sarah Orne Jewett, her more artistic successor, she had sharp eyes to see an effective means to indicate the flavor of the regional life.

On these terms, given by nature, she could not fail. Just as among her first apprentice sketches the most successful are those about New England, so her later novels of New England have a liveliness unmatched elsewhere in her writings. But even so, the reader must not expect too much. Although she was one of the best-informed and most interesting interpreters of New England, Mrs. Stowe was neither accurate nor complete, for disinterested objectivity was no part of her principles. Characteristically enough, she threw most of her stories out of perspective by dating them a few years before her birth, so that they occur in an idealized wonderland midway between her own experience and the visions of Cotton Mather.

A brief example of her selectivity is afforded by her sketch "The First Christmas in New England," as it appeared in the *Christian Union*. After describing the approach of the *Mayflower* ship to the Cape Cod country, she gives an imaginative account of how the holy day was spent. According to her, not only Christmas but the entire period was filled mainly with hymn-singing, preaching, and pious conversations; the labor of constructing new homes and of protecting them from the dispossessed Indians was thrust into the background. Her Puritans are entirely too other-worldly to fit Governor Bradford's account of a Pilgrim Christmas. As he describes the day, it was spent, like all others, in godly labor, except by malingerers who were not adverse to shirking their responsibilities or fooling the authorities.

In Cotton Mather (1663-1728) Mrs. Stowe found an old master best suited to be the pattern of her conceptions. From her girlhood she loved him; his temperament, unfailingly pleasant to her, she described as that of "a delightful old New

England grandmother," to which her own reverberated gently and gratefully.² One need read very little of Mather's *Magnalia* or of his *Wonders of the Invisible World* before discovering the basis of her fondness, for Mather offers the same conception of the New England people as hers. They are, or at least were, the salt of the earth: "The world will do New England a great piece of Injustice, if it acknowledge not a measure of Religion, Loyalty, Honesty, and Industry, in the People there, beyond what is to be found with any other People for the Number of them. . . . New England was a true Utopia."³

II *Oldtown Folks (1869)*

Mrs. Stowe wrote four complete books about New England life, in addition to a number of sketches, most of them collected in the unfortunate, unread *Mayflower* (1843) and in *Oldtown Fireside Stories* (1872). Her first important volume, the same *Mayflower*, and her last important one, *Poganuc People* (1878), were New England to the core; her most important volume, *Oldtown Folks*, exhaled the very spirit of the region; and two other successful novels, *The Minister's Wooing* (1859) and *The Pearl of Orr's Island* (1862), owed their success largely to the flavor of New England in them. Upon these six books, in the last analysis, Mrs. Stowe's reputation as a writer must rest rather than upon the gorgeous, unpredicted success of *Uncle Tom's Cabin*.

By far most comprehensive of these New England novels, her own favorite among them, and indeed the best book she ever wrote is *Oldtown Folks* in which she combined her husband's memories of his youth with her own dreams. Among all of her works, it is the book to be read with the maximum of quiet enjoyment and the minimum of exasperation. In it there is less of obvious falsification than in her other works, and though it would not bear the test of rigorous formal analysis any more successfully than they, it is less tempting to the analytical-critical mind. By disarming criticism, *Oldtown Folks* turns the attention from artistic improprieties to human relationships.

That it gives a too-rosy description of New England life at the end of the eighteenth century is undeniable, but the description, imaginatively convincing, is also at least plausible historically. Americans were an industrious, religious, prosperous people then, still tolerably unspoiled and modest. Within limitations, some Americans possessed the virtues that Americans like to consider as belonging to them all without limitation. *Oldtown Folks* is both, in its social setting, the most realistic of Mrs. Stowe's fiction and, in the persuasiveness of its illusion, the most imaginative.

The story, told by Horace Holyoke, relates the events of his youth in Massachusetts. This visionary lad, his visions patterned after Calvin Stowe's, having been left an orphan in early childhood, is reared in his grandparents' family in the normal regime of schooling, farming, churchgoing. But into the town and the family wander two other orphans, waifs, the boy Harry and his magnetic sister Tina, with whom the plot has most to do. Though Mrs. Stowe treated Tina as the principal character, she felt as contemptuous towards the beautiful, fascinating temptress as ever George Eliot did to one of her physically attractive and mentally uninteresting young creatures. In reaction, Mrs. Stowe finally married the girl to the narrator Horace; but she did so only after Tina's foolish, vain marriage with a Byronic intriguer—a veritable Aaron Burr—which had chastened her by a decade of suffering and humiliation. Enabled by this thread of her story to introduce descriptions of the Boston gentry, she was allowed to throw greater glamor over the Oldtown people, only an easy three hours' carriage ride from Boston but a whole age removed into pastoral, idyllic life.

Whoever wants to learn from fiction what the immediate descendants of the Puritans were before the coming of transcendentalism and the factory system need look no further than *Oldtown Folks.* They are shown—to some degree intentionally—in their self-will and self-righteousness, their hardheartedness, their emotional starvation, and their simple snobbery. They are exhibited with their admixture of bloodcurdling religion and practical charity and sympathy. The merriment of their life is revealed, as are their peaceful sleeping during the long Sunday wastes of sermon and prayers, the pranks of the children at church, and their inescapable scoldings about which nobody cared.

Finely colored as the descriptions of the country are, with its beautiful yellow days leading into the harsh winter, Mrs. Stowe excelled them in her account of how the people were living during the administrations of President Washington and his immediate successors. As no tourist or visitor can, she takes her reader into their houses with their giant kitchen fireplaces and their musty parlors, and she lets him see them eating their beans and salt pork, taking their snuff, and drinking their cider. She initiates him into the mysteries of the weekend bath, the vigorous washings that used to make Saturday nights a terror to children of good families.

Nor was Mrs. Stowe forgetful of the limitations of this life, desirable as she considered it to be. She liked the dominance given to the preacher in town, for he, the leading aristocrat, was followed by the other learned men; but she disliked the strong old-fashioned doctrine of President Jonathan Edwards and of Wigglesworth's *Day of Doom,* which she regarded as being monarchical and un-American. There were certain improvements in the original model that she had worked out for herself, though she found them also in the Church of England. What pleased her most was the people's habit of arranging their views to suit their practices: the doctrines may have been hard, but the lives were merry.

Only one embarrassing feature of their beliefs does she skip over gingerly: their superstitions. Aside from the mild visions of Horace (in some of which Tina's mother comes and guides him) and the ghost that appears to old Crab Smith, there is absolute silence about the rich vein of popular lore that, having produced the witch hunts of previous generations, left its trail curling through the lives of all.

The fifteen local color sketches reprinted from the *Atlantic Monthly* and the *Christian Union* as *Sam Lawson's Oldtown Fireside Stories* (1872) are more closely connected with *Oldtown Folks* in name than in scope or weight. Sam had been introduced early in the novel as "the village do-nothing," the keen Yankee jack-of-all-trades whose particular delight was spinning yarns—in dialect. After the novel was finished, enough of Calvin Stowe's yarns were on hand to fill a volume. They are the stories—comic or serious, but always edifying—that Sam told the boys, usually on their Saturday afternoon rambles.

The moral reflections, inserted with unremitting premeditation, differed from those of *My Wife and I* principally in the dialect: "Lordy massy! riches allers covers a multitude o' sins" (48); "There's a consid'able sight o' gumption in grandmas" (140); "Folks never does see nothin' when they aint' lookin' where 'tis" (153). Gentle satire is not completely lacking: "Folks allers preaches betters on the vanity o' riches when they's in tol'able easy circumstances" (136). But no satire is intended in passages like this: "Wal, ye see that 'are's the way fellers allers begin the ways o' sin, by turnin' their back on the Bible and the advice o' pious parents" (106-7).[4]

III   *The Final Word*: Poganuc People *(1878)*

The true successor to Calvin Stowe's reminiscences is *Poganuc People;* written about a decade later, it is a fictionalized account of Mrs. Stowe's own childhood. The Poganuc of the book is Litchfield; the minister, Lyman Beecher; and Dolly Cushman, Harriet Beecher. So many changes have been introduced, however, that only in spirit can the heroine be a representation of Harriet, who did not, as Dolly does in the story, marry a young man from Oxford University and settle down to the life of a Boston matron. And strangely enough, another alteration consisted of imagining Dolly to be the youngest child in the family, thus eliminating all reference to Henry Ward Beecher. The scene which biographers love to reproduce, the ransacking of the barrels of theological tracts in the attic, followed by the discovery of the *Arabian Nights,* appears here in full detail (170 ff.).

As the story opens Dolly is a little girl, the youngest of the ten children of the poor parson. The parents are opposed on principle to paying too much apparent attention to a child; and Dolly, who feels that she is commonly in the adults' way, continually "sighed over the dreadful insignificance of being only a little girl in a great family of grown-up people" (17). Because the father is too deeply engrossed with theology and the mother slightly ineffectual, Dolly longs in vain for sympathetic personal attention; she likes to imagine herself as either dead or grown up; and, when she has a cold, she is glad of it because of the importance it gives her.

Weary as the author of *Poganuc People* obviously was by 1878, some of the scenes are charming; and, as in *Oldtown Folks,* a real human interest lies in the spirit of old days when people so like and so unlike Americans today muddled their curious ways through life. And those readers who regret the absence of art in the story should remember that for Mrs. Stowe art was vanity; in her vocabulary "work of art," as she reminded them, was nothing beyond "a hackneyed modern expression" (241).

To the analyst of Mrs. Stowe's character, *Poganuc People* holds the special interest inherent in her memories of her father. Though she tried desperately to be just to him, she was unable to conceal her grievances. Thus, in the story, the reformation of Zeph Higgins, a self-willed, hardhearted misfit, is not the direct result of the preacher's exhortations. When Mrs. Higgins dies, she beseeches Zeph to reconcile himself to the church; but the hardened sinner, though he attends services, becomes increasingly certain that he is doomed to damnation. He is indeed a challenge to the church, but the preacher declines the struggle for his soul, saying that only God can speak to such a stubborn heart as Zeph's. God chooses to speak through Dolly, and old Zeph, reborn in grace through her, becomes Uncle Zeph, beloved by the whole town.[5]

Thus did Mrs. Stowe, at the mature age of sixty-seven, declare the advantage of her religion of love over her father's religion of law; from early childhood, she asserted, she could have performed the Lord's work better than he. Such passages were the concluding skirmishes of her campaign against Jonathan Edwards, the great theological rival of her favorite Cotton Mather and the perpetual terror of her girlish religious gropings. On Edwards himself she had already wreaked what must have appealed to her as full, though tolerant revenge. Two of her villains—in *Oldtown Folks* and *The Minister's Wooing*—are specifically described as Edwards' grandsons, the inevitable wicked fruits of false doctrines. Nor did her vengeance stop with these hints. "It was his power and his influence," she stated in *Oldtown Folks,* "which succeeded in completely upsetting New England . . . and casting out of the Church the children of the very saints and martyrs who had come to this country for no other reason than to found a church" (364).

To invective against Edwards she added the device of *reductio ad absurdum* in the person of a follower who, ruthlessly torturing his congregation with the sense of their unmitigated depravity, was privately "an artless, simple-hearted, gentle-mannered man" who "wore two holes in the floor opposite his table in the spot where year after year his feet were placed in study." Thus she worked out the complete justification for rejecting her father's views: the saints had been driven from the church in which the only escape from horrible false doctrines was the inability to believe them.

This mellow understanding is the very essence of those portions of *Poganuc People* in which, on more than one occasion, she permits herself innocent quips at Lyman Beecher's expense. In one place, after he has been discussing free will and divine agency with a puzzled parishioner and settling the matter to his own satisfaction, she comments: "Having thus wound up the sun and moon, and arranged the courses of the stars in celestial regions, the Doctor was as alert and light-hearted as any boy, in his preparations for the day's enterprise" (223). His absent-mindedness became, in another facetious description, "a little habit of departing unceremoniously into some celestial region of thought in the midst of conversation." It was, to be sure, a pardonable weakness; but this similar inability to enter into the life of his young daughter, though also pardonable, never ceased to arouse her resentment. She found herself apologizing for him, for two reasons: he had never been a mother, and he had never understood true Christianity.

IV *Two Other New England Novels*

Of Mrs. Stowe's two other New England stories, first published as serials in the *Atlantic Monthly* and the *Independent,* the minor work, *The Pearl of Orr's Island* (1862), is now the more agreeable reading. In its day, however, *The Minister's Wooing* (1859) was more famous. It had the publicity advantages of James Russell Lowell's editorial endorsement, of subsequent controversy over historical and doctrinal accuracy, and of the use of the Beecher archives, to which several of the family biographers have referred. Such circumstances have given the book undue prominence, especially since its intrinsic merits as a chronicle of New England have been more fully revealed in its successor by a dozen years, *Oldtown Folks*.

The Pearl of Orr's Island stands apart from Mrs. Stowe's other stories, since in it, the only time in her works, she exploited the achievements of the New England sailors. The opening pages, in fact, are unusually charming, and Sarah Orne Jewett has spoken admiringly of them in an autobiographical preface to *Deephaven*, expressing deep gratitude for the book's revelation to her, a young girl, of "those who dwelt along the wooded seacoast and by the decaying, shipless harbors" of her native state. To a degree, this charm persists, but only to a degree, for the development of the story does not fulfill the high promise of the start. As Miss Jewett wrote, on another occasion, in a letter to Mrs. Fields, "Alas, that she couldn't finish it in the same noble key of simplicity and harmony."[6]

Basically, the plot of *The Pearl of Orr's Island* is no more complicated than most of Mrs. Stowe's ingenuous fables: the love of a gentle, matronly child for a headstrong, wild youth concludes with the death of the girl and the spiritual awakening of the young man. The complications are the youth's struggle with his pride, and the thoughtless rivalry of a flirting neighbor girl; but the native nobility of all three is sufficient guarantee of the happy solution. For is not death a happy solution? Mrs. Stowe asks, using the demise of the saintly Mara as an opportunity to expound the true Christian attitude towards death. Other inescapable asides concern spiritualism, the divine inspiration of the Bible, and, at great length, the proper education of children.[7]

This last problem is more intimately connected with the story than might be suspected, for Moses, the young hero, is, if the truth be told, a problem child. Not only is he a waif and an orphan, washed upon the Maine coast by a storm; but he is the son of parents who were rich, Catholic, Southern, and, in part, Spanish—a combination of handicaps for which the only hope is rigorous education in a New England sea-captain's God-fearing family. The task requires all the force of Mara's motherly love (developed in her before she was thirteen) and all the "innocent hypocrisy" and "gentle vindictiveness" which Mrs. Stowe specifies as two saintly and womanly virtues (229, 246).

To make the treatment stick, the emphasis of Mara's death is required; and so Mrs. Stowe leaves Moses, master of his own ship, a neophyte in prayer, and the husband of the little flirt next door, now also chastened and sobered into nobility. The moral is clear: the American chosen people, with their harsh visages but tender hearts, were able as a group to mold the "real wild ass's colt" into a presentable imitation of a little Beecher Calvinist.

A simple tale? *The Minister's Wooing,* except for more important characters involved, is hardly less simple: a conventional situation, the love of three men for a girl, is resolved without surprises. Of the heroine, Mary Scudder, a small town jewel, it need but be said that, like Mara, she is a model of Christian girlhood, and the nearest approach to an angel to be found on this earth. The desirous males include Dr. Samuel Hopkins, a divine well known in his day; Colonel Aaron Burr, well known in this era; and young James, a lad entirely fictional, the lucky suitor. Thus there are really three wooings in the story, and the plot is not difficult to foresee.

Objected to by the girl's mother, James goes to sea and is apparently drowned in a shipwreck, with his salvation in doubt because of his incomplete acceptance of Christianity. Colonel Burr, arriving in town on a visit, can not resist the temptation to flirt with gentle Mary. The Puritan maiden— Mrs. Stowe is fond of applying the adjective to eighteenth-century New Englanders—finally gives him an edifying lecture and, simultaneously, his walking-papers, thus leaving the way clear for the minister.

Doctor Hopkins is a fairly concrete character. Mrs. Stowe, who knew preachers from *a* to *z*, introduced into her portrait a large share of her father's theology and a number of her husband's character traits. The learned, good man—utterly without imagination or what is commonly understood as romance— lives in the world of high idealism and biblical citation. His wooing proper consists in asking Mary's mother, who would be a much better match for him, whether the girl will accept him. When the offer is brought to Mary, she has no need to feign surprise. Resigned to God's will, after her sufferings over her sweetheart's supposed death, she resolves to marry the minister to gratify her mother and him. "When we renounce self in anything," she confides to James's mother, anticipating Christopher Crowfield, "we have reason to hope for God's blessings; and so I feel assured of a peaceful life in the course I have taken" (458).

With no higher hopes than these, she is rudely upset by the return of James, full of love, Christian now through his parting conversations with her, and incidentally rich. Duty, of course, is to carry her through marriage with the minister; but Miss Prissy Diamond, the village dressmaker and know-it-all, taking matters into her own hands, reveals to the good minister where his fiancée's heart lies, and the necessary sacrifice becomes his instead of Mary's.

James and Mary are united: "The fair poetic maiden, the seeress, the saint, has passed into that appointed shrine for woman, more holy than cloister, more saintly and pure than church or altar—a *Christian home.*"[8] Eventually, a sentence informs the readers, good Doctor Hopkins marries a "woman of fair countenance" who presents him with sons and daughters.

A typical product of Mrs. Stowe's mind, *The Minister's Wooing* inevitably repeats a good many of her pet ideas. She regarded any good woman as a better evangelist than the greatest divine; and the scene in which Colonel Aaron Burr, listening to a lecture on his sins delivered by Mary, breaks down and weeps is doubly unbelievable in its simplicity (478).

The minister whose futile, undignified courtship was thus circumstantially disclosed was the historic and celebrated Dr. Samuel Hopkins, whose biography had been written shortly before by Dr. Park, president of the seminary at Andover in which Dr. Stowe was teaching. Disturbed by the theological, geographical, and biographical inaccuracies in her story as it appeared serially in the *Atlantic,* Dr. Park urged the author to correct her errors before allowing publication in book form, a well meant suggestion which, as he might have been forewarned, she refused to consider; Mrs. Stowe had a fine scorn of mere literal accuracy.[9]

In comparison with *Oldtown Folks, The Minister's Wooing* suffers from thinness of detail; and yet, since the book appeared about ten years earlier, when *Oldtown Folks* followed it was inevitably criticized adversely for its similarities to its forerunner. Thus Mrs. Florine McCray, the first unauthorized biographer, complained of "a poverty of invention" in *Oldtown Folks,* specifying, in addition to repetitions within the book itself, the reincarnation of Mrs. Stowe's typical minister (attributed by her to Lyman Beecher) and her typical schoolmaster (John P. Brace) under the thin disguise of new names. Mrs. McCray also regretted the reappearance of Mrs. Marvyn as Esther Avery, and the awkward entrance of "a cousin" of Aaron Burr to imitate that gentleman's fascinating villainies. Such objections, well founded as they are, need never bother the reader who takes a friendly hint to postpone indefinitely his reading of *The Minister's Wooing* in favor of a glance at *Oldtown Folks.*[10]

The curious may find an interest in a little story for children, "The Minister's Watermelons." In it William Somers, an academy boy, tells how he fell in love with fellow student Lucy Sewell; and, under the domination of an older boy, Elliot Vinton, stole her father's melons and confessed his fault. The psychological relationship is a repetition of that in *Oldtown Folks* between Horace, Tina, and the Byronic Ellery Davenport.

V *Italy Fails the Test*

Italy, which had fascinated and thrilled Mrs. Stowe on her third memorable European journey, fell far short of her ideal of Christian propriety. As might be expected from her anti-Catholic prejudices, she was near her weakest in *Agnes of Sorrento* (1862), the Italian romance. Exotic Italy, which tested the penetration of Hawthorne in *The Marble Faun* and the political acumen of James Fenimore Cooper in *The Bravo,* hurled her to ignominious defeat. With no great cause to inspire her and no inbred traditions to lend body to her work, she had little left but romantic tricks and a limitless supply of Beecher prejudices. *Agnes of Sorrento* is therefore one of the most personal of her works, and one of the most provincial. It is more restrictedly New England than *Oldtown Folks;* and in its lack of historical perspective it is anything other than what its title page professes: "an historical novel of the time of Savonarola."

The book, though originating in the delight Mrs. Stowe felt in Italy, is filled with her inbred deprecation of Catholic customs, Catholic doctrines, and even of Italy itself. "Our enlightened Protestantism" enabled her to be charitable: "Let us not, from the height of our day with the better appliances which a universal press gives us, sneer at the homely rounds of the ladder by which the first multitudes of the Lord's flock climbed heavenward."[11]

Consequently, she never sneered; she was content to patronize. She sorrowed at the thought of "these good women," the Catholic sisters, "unwittingly deprived of any power of making comparisons, or ever having Christ's sweetest parable of the heavenly kingdom enacted in homes of their own." She relegated to its proper place "a picture of the Crucifixion by Fra Angelico; which, whatever might be its *naive* defects of drawing and perspective, had an intense earnestness of feeling." The piety and the sincerity of the artist she found, undoubtedly, more worthy of note for their relative absence throughout the greater part of Italian life. "In fact," she generalized, "the climate of Southern Italy and its gorgeous scenery are more favorable to voluptuous ecstasy than to the severe and grave warfare of the true Christian soldier." And the uppers of the boot, she suspected, were of no better material than the toe.[12]

The story takes its name from the heroine, the beautiful young girl Agnes, whom everyone loved—as was the case of Eva St. Clare—and who was favored or afflicted, like Tina or Mary Scudder, by three particular adorers. One, the candidate advanced by her grandmother Elsie, was a simple clod, named Antonio—but there are no peasants in New England; second, her father confessor Francesco—contrast the poor soul with Dr. Hopkins—driven nigh to insanity by his guilty passion; and third, the young cavalier Prince Agostino Sarelli, eventually the lucky man. The love story, a mere excuse, was as usual far removed from the author's main interest; for, since the corruption in the Catholic Church fascinated her, she found herself almost unconsciously writing a tract.

She used Savonarola, the central historical character, as "an Italian Luther" and she praised the Florentines as "the Puritans of Italy." By means of these comparisons she was able to sweep aside the Catholicism of both the Pope and Savonarola; and also her father's stern New England Protestantism—all contrasted unfavorably with a nebulous, undefinable religion of Love.

Her technique in discussing Catholicism was the same as in discussing slavery: with no concern for traditions or facts, she asked herself what the possible types of misconduct were; and she was sure that, if they could exist, they did. From this consideration she built what she thought was a truthful image of the institution at its worst. For the other side of the picture she assumed, as far as permitted by her knowledge of human frailty, that the ideals of the institution were occasionally achieved. From this contrast of opposites she derived a story which was strongly melodramatic and should have been, in this instance, much more exciting than it turned out to be.

Defective imagination rather than defective thinking made *Agnes of Sorrento* commonplace. Consistent with her habit, she introduced young Agostino, a dissolute Byronist like Ellery Davenport and Aaron Burr, who sought to seduce the fair, pure maiden by flattery and jewelry; but she thought better of him by the ninth chapter and altered his past to transform him into a victim of oppression. Finally reconciling herself to him, in spite of his Italian blood, she made him as one with herself: his "blind sense of personal injury" had been converted into a "fixed principle of moral indignation and opposition" (349). Equally lacking in consistent development is the character of Il Padre Francesco, who is alternately enlightened and superstitious, progressive and reactionary.

Mrs. Stowe was on the whole rather too casual with her characters. She did not follow them as closely as trained readers demand. She said about one of them, Antonio as it happened, "We may have introduced him to the reader before, who likely enough has forgotten by this time our portraiture; so we shall say again . . ." (227). Evidently she herself was not sure whether she had mentioned Antonio; the matter was of slight importance to her, and she obviously expected her readers to have no greater interest in him than she had. She never decided upon the status of her hero; she described him as penniless and without influence but almost simultaneously referred to his wealthy and powerful relatives. The women fared somewhat better. The heroine Agnes was consistently made the mouthpiece of the author's religion of love, and two older women were allowed to utter many homely truths in the manner of New England crones freely speaking their minds.

VI *Florida*

It is indeed pleasantly restful to turn from this misconceived Italian romance to the humbler pages of *Palmetto-Leaves* (1873), a book of sketches about Florida which shows a more successful escape. In Mandarin, a very small town on the St. Johns River near Jacksonville, where Mrs. Stowe had settled in the late 1860's, she found the joy of a foreign country without the bewilderment of violent change. Her primary purpose in moving South she characteristically stated as a desire to improve the Negroes by providing education and Episcopalianism for their "immature minds." That kind soul her husband held services for both white and colored folks; but as she was kept very busy with her writing, her own charities were more likely to be on behalf of organizations or of individuals who could be reached by mail. She was highly pleased by the piety and industry of the Negroes around her, seeing them "very happy in their lowly lot" and—pleasing her equally— "growing richer and richer."[13]

But all such benevolent reform became, as time passed, incidental. In her deep, almost pathetic attachment to the calm South, her joy in her Florida winter home was produced less by any help she might give than by that she was unquestionably receiving. Primarily, she was happy in a new way because she was being withdrawn from the troubles of active life; and as one contemplates this happiness he is tempted to subscribe to the generalization that the North is fit only for frenzied activity and the South for civilized living.

Although Mrs. Stowe was herself only a partial exemplification of this doubtful truth, her Florida home was in a striking way the nearest her life ever approached to a center of quiet. "The world that hates Christ" was eliminated from Mandarin, her "calm isle of Patmos" (AF, 343). There she could write her three hours a day when she was able, or spend a winter reading lives of Christ and thanking God she was one of the elect. She felt herself protected from "these sensational days," as she wrote Oliver Wendell Holmes in 1879, in which "heaven and earth seemed to be racked for a thrill" (AF, 373). She never doubted the favor of her Lord, and it was only an extension of her faith that led to her declaration that she had not written *Uncle Tom's Cabin*. "I did not write it," she told one of her neighbors. "God wrote it. I merely did his dictation" (AF, 377).

Upon occasion she withdrew voluntarily from this haven of rest, as for a speaking tour in the fall and winter of 1872-73; and she was drawn unwillingly from it at other times, as by the charge of adultery brought against her brother by his young friend, Theodore Tilton, in 1874. Though her faith in Henry Ward never wavered, the strain of the protracted trial and the distasteful notoriety accompanying it damaged her health, perhaps permanently. To her mind, the proceedings against Henry Ward were a clear case of the world against Christ. Her faith in him remained unshaken, but legal expenses of one hundred and eighteen thousand dollars were a form of the Lord's chastening that she had never courted.[14]

Only slightly less personal than her letters from these years are the sketches for the *Christian Union* published in 1873 as *Palmetto-Leaves*. They show how within half a decade she had adapted herself to the physical life of the Old South, and how remarkably she had identified her interests with those of Florida. "Your Northern snowstorms . . . hold back our springs" was one of her complaints against her erstwhile fellow-Yanks; and she shuddered at an invitation to revisit Cincinnati. The accusation that the state of Florida consisted of nine-tenths water and one-tenth swamp deeply hurt her. The malarial fevers, she responded, were mild compared with those of New York and New England; and for the deadly moccasin snake she found no stronger adjective than "unsavory."[15]

She liked almost everything in Florida, and a perpetual song of joy fills the pages of the book. Like a missionary in the field, Mrs. Stowe sent her glowing reports North. Incidentally, she was collecting money for her private charity, the church and school at Mandarin; but she was filled with zeal for the whole Jacksonville-St. Johns River region. Practical woman that she was, she answered questions about the price of board at the winter resorts—it ranged from eight to thirty-five dollars a week—and about the price of land—there was good land at from one to five dollars an acre. She gave definite instructions about clothes, summarized the techniques of producing oranges and preserving figs, and described the flora of the region in copious detail. Above all, though, it was the glorious climate that she expatiated upon, eloquently testifying to its value for the aged as well as for invalids and children.

In adjusting herself to this new life, she showed greater power of adaptation than could have been suspected in an old Yankee. She learned not to expect all of the exactitude of New England; she patiently took cognizance of what could or could not be demanded. Hard experience taught her the difference between a Negress brought up in the fields and one educated as a house servant; and, instead of complaining that Negroes were lazy, she was amazed at the work they could accomplish under a hot sun that would have been, so she thought, a white man's death. She regarded them as already the best labor in the South; and, when *carefully looked over* (she italicized the phrase), she found them as productive as any laborers that could be hired in the North and more obedient and more easily satisfied (315). The reconstructed state of Florida, as she finally saw it, was a nearer approach to God's country than New England, outside of Cotton Mather's pages, had ever revealed itself to her.

The people of Florida liked her and Calvin Stowe as well as she liked them. To be sure, there were occasional impoliteness and insult to be borne, such as persons refusing to remain in church with the Stowes; but these were more than outweighed by formal receptions in her honor and by the obvious gratitude felt toward both Mrs. Stowe and her husband. As the local history of Mandarin shows, she was the small town's leading citizen and is still its principal claim to attention. To some of her neighbors she was only a kindly lady with a dimly famous name—the era of *Uncle Tom's Cabin* was so far in the past—and the literate ones accepted her as if she were a convert eager to repair through good works the damage she had done in the past.

Palmetto-Leaves and her magazine articles—the best publicity imaginable, unsolicited, free and palpably sincere—were a strong argument in her favor. The writings not only brought tourists, but the author herself was a tourist attraction. Stereoscopic views of the Stowes on their veranda and on the spacious lawn in front of their home were sold nationally. A navigation company, which instituted round-trip excursions up the St. Johns River from Jacksonville to Mandarin, guaranteed a view of the Stowe orange grove and optimistically hinted at opportunities to see the celebrities also. Though the tourists were sometimes a nuisance to the Stowes, they were an asset to the community.[16]

Whatever Mrs. Stowe may have intended to do for education and religion in Florida when she settled there, it is clear that she reaped the benefits of her move in improved health and peace. She had discovered that the South, if properly colonized by Episcopalians, could be kept as free from debauchery and debasing vice as the North; and it offered the added inducement to true godliness of a mild and tolerant climate. Increasing age, unfortunately, and decreasing mental activity obscured this true moral of geography. Her immigration into God's country of the soul had been too long delayed by frantic diggings into the stony wastes of New England. Quite idyllic, however one looks at it, was her escape from New England, the domain of a justly stern and angry God, into the mildness of Florida, the creation of love and pity. In spite of all her rebellion, the universe had accepted her: the South was the triumph of her life, the accidental fulfillment of her dreams.

CHAPTER 7

Magazinist

I A Network of Names

THE SIXTEEN VOLUMES of *The Writings of Harriet Beecher Stowe*, in the handsome uniform bindings provided by Houghton Mifflin and Company, have been beautified like exhibits of wild animals in natural history museums. Selected specimens, carefully stuffed and curried, stand stiffly in display cases embellished with equally careful selections from the flora and minor fauna of their environment. In the magazine files, covered with the dust of years and undisturbed by editorial ablutions, one finds a closer approach to the living beast in his jungle. Here lie the literary achievements of Mrs. Stowe with the background preserved as it appeared to her original readers —for it was to the magazines that she made her first appeal, and it was through their columns, after *Uncle Tom's Cabin*, that her name was most regularly kept before her public.

Hence the magazines, for her more than for most writers, are primary sources of study. When one recalls further how much of what she wrote for them never reached book publication, their significance is inescapable. Most important, the magazines show more clearly the continuity of her career. A network of names connects one magazine with another, revealing the links between one of her enterprises and the next.

One should consider, for example, her connections with religious publications. In the beginning were the Cincinnati *Journal*, with Henry Ward Beecher as editor *pro tem.*, and the New York *Evangelist*, with Joshua Leavitt and George Cheever among the editors. When Mrs. Stowe left the *Evangelist* for the *Independent*, one of the editors of the *Independent* was Joshua Leavitt, and the star contributors were George Cheever and

Henry Ward Beecher. The latter also served intermittently, either in name or fact, as editor of the *Independent*. When Mrs. Stowe left the *Independent* for the *Christian Union*, the editor and chief mainstay of the latter was Henry Ward Beecher, and Cheever remained as an occasional contributor.

In her secular writing, the *Western Monthly Magazine* began a broader development, and yet even here Miss Gould and Mrs. Hentz turned up very soon in *Godey's Lady's Book* and in the gift annuals, where Mrs. Sigourney and Miss Sedgwick—incidentally big names in the reprints of the Cincinnati *Chronicle*—held full sway. The *Lady's Book* also printed small quantities of Longfellow and Holmes, later to be so important in the *Atlantic Monthly*.

The *National Era*, Mrs. Stowe's first abolitionist contact, preserved some of the old names, as well as adding important new ones such as· Whittier and Lowell. When the *Atlantic* began, Lowell was at its head; and the name of Whittier appeared with Mrs. Stowe's beside others even more eminent. Whittier also made the move with her from the *National Era* to the *Independent*. An *Atlantic* contributor, Edward Everett Hale, bought her work for his own journal *Old and New;* and his name also reappeared in the columns of the *Christian Union,* a curious evangelical setting for his calm Unitarianism.

The story of these interlocking names would be endless. The Cary sisters, Alice and Phoebe, from Cincinnati, followed her through the annuals, the *Lady's Book,* the *National Era,* the *Independent,* and the *Christian Union.* James T. Fields, a contributor with her to several annuals ·and to the *Lady's Book,* took her to his *Our Young Folks*—and incidentally to her biographer and devoted friend, his wife. Lucy Larcom, one of the editors of his magazine, had already crossed Mrs. Stowe's path in the *National Era,* while other contributors to *Our Young Folks* were also, like her, writing for the *Atlantic* under the same publisher.

Certain major figures, like Whitman, she touched hardly at all; but her writings appeared in the same magazines with those of Poe and Henry James. With her two styles—the one vividly fresh and encouraged by James Hall, the other sentimentally devotional and encouraged by her family tradition— she spread widely. One might say that what was fresh about her writing stemmed from Yankee wit aided by the perspective of Cincinnati and the West and that the more stodgy didactic parts are in the tradition of the evangelical group to which her family belonged.

Along with these literary names, the Beechers appear everywhere. E. D. Mansfield, editor of the *Chronicle*, had been a member of Lyman Beecher's congregation in Litchfield, and regarded him as the greatest American preacher. John B. Ford, the publisher of the *Christian Union*, was a member of Henry Ward Beecher's congregation in Brooklyn, and regarded him as the greatest American preacher. Catherine was not only Harriet's early collaborator, but followed her through the annuals, the magazines devoted to the position of women, and, at an advanced age, into the *Christian Union*. In the church publications from the Cincinnati *Journal* on, her brother and her husband played their minor or major parts—and she pushed Calvin Stowe into the *Atlantic* and even into *Godey's Lady's Book* with a solemn article on the Thanksgiving holiday.

This endless chain of Mrs. Stowe's associates defines her literary environment; and, with some links observed in detail, it throws light upon her week-by-week work. To observe the magazines for which she did most in her later years following *Uncle Tom's Cabin* is to show her as she was. The *Independent*, *Hearth and Home*, and the *Christian Union* are the most significant, each in its own way, of this essential aspect of her work.

II *The* Independent

In 1852, when Mrs. Stowe joined the staff, the *Independent* was a four-page weekly newspaper or magazine like the *Evangelist*, in policy as well as appearance. The *Independent* described itself as "conducted by pastors of Congregational churches," with Leonard Bacon, Joseph P. Thomson and Joshua Leavitt as editors, and with Henry Ward Beecher (liberal) and George B. Cheever (conservative) as signed contributors—more properly, as contributing editors. On July 1, 1852, Mrs. Stowe was listed as a third special correspondent, a position she held for ten years. During the remainder of 1852 and 1853, she sent the *Independent* nothing essential; her contribution consisted of the story "How to Make Friends with Mammon," later reprinted in *The May Flower* of 1855, some verse, the letters of the Stowe-Parker libel controversy, and some chapters from *A Key to Uncle Tom's Cabin*, printed in advance of the book. During this period, the magazine carried many stories about her and the progress of *Uncle Tom's Cabin*, but for over a year, including the whole of 1853, she sent nothing although her name was carried as a contributor.

In 1854—the paper had meantime expanded to eight pages— she was more active. One of her pieces, "An Appeal to the Women of the Free States," was a plea that they work for the abolition of slavery. The others were a series of ten articles, called "Shadows on the Hebrew Mountains"; these were lay sermons on piety, faith, and resignation, with such morals as "give up the temptations of the world" and "afflictions are for man's good—but not necessarily good in themselves." The "Shadows," which have never been reprinted, are in the style— which she had already begun in the *Evangelist*—later displayed fully in *Footsteps of the Master*.

During 1857 she sent to the *Independent* four "Letters from Europe," one dated from Rome, the other three from Paris, in the general vein of the earlier *Sunny Memories of Foreign Lands*. Their general tone, already familiar from *Sunny Memories*, can be gathered from a single sentence: "Our liberty is built on our religion, and the same religion would give France the same liberty" (January 9). By "our liberty" she meant English and American, and by "our religion" she meant Protestantism. Her other articles for 1857 were lay sermons, "How Jesus Loved Mary and her Sister," "Things that Cannot be Shaken," and "Who shall roll away the Stone?" This last (September 3), the most interesting of the three, repeated her demand for an unquestionable angel, not the doubtful shades of spiritualism.

In 1858 there was more verse; some stories like "Our Charley" (reprinted in the *Writings*), four unreprinted essays in defense of revivals, one against the Jesuits, one calling attention to the achievements of Negroes, a suggestion for indoor decoration, and an appeal to the churches to come out strongly against slavery. These have more force and vitality than most of her writings for the *Independent,* and they furnish a good cross-section of her interests at the time.

The spring of 1859 finds only two articles on "The Higher Christian Life," but in December of that year begins a series of letters from Europe. Twenty-three in all, they ran from December 1, 1859, to August 23, 1860. They are fully equal to *Sunny Memories*, and it is probable that they would have been worked over into a book had not the Civil War kept the interests of the readers nearer home. The material of these letters is the basis for her later inferior series for the New York *Ledger* in 1865.

On her return to this country, Mrs. Stowe sent the *Independent* six more articles during 1860. These include a friendly note on the visit of British royalty, one of her now rare moral tales, two more articles urging the churches to take a stronger stand, an attack upon President Buchanan, and an editorial rejoicing in Lincoln's election: "We are aware that the Republican Party are far from being up to the full measure of what *ought* to be thought and felt on the slavery question. But they are for *stopping the evil*—and in this case to arrest is to cure. . . . Meanwhile, the friends of anti-slavery principle should not relax labor" ("What Hath God Wrought," Nov. 15).

In 1861 Mrs. Stowe began her serial story, *The Pearl of Orr's Island*, but it was suspended after seventeen chapters and resumed only after a lapse of seven months. For shorter articles, requiring less concentration, she wrote "Getting ready for a Gale," one week after Fort Sumter had been bombarded, and several denunciations of her old enemy the London *Times* and defenses of the good will of the English people. The following year she wound up her connection with the *Independent* in a series of six articles combining biblical stories with an appeal for immediate emancipation of the Negroes. Throughout them she necessarily took issue with President Lincoln over his desire to save the Union at whatever cost. The abolition of slavery, she kept insisting, was the first duty of a Christian commonwealth.

Mrs. Stowe's association with the *Independent*, during the decade between 1852 and 1862, was not especially propitious; but it did produce, in some of her travel letters and later political editorials, articles that merited inclusion in the main body of her collected *Writings*. Too often she wrote as if fumbling for a subject, probably because her main interests were with *Dred,*

The Minister's Wooing, Agnes of Sorrento, or other writing she was doing. Fate was against her too, for during such crises as the Dred Scott excitement and John Brown's raid, she was in Europe and unable to express quickly enough the indignation that she felt. George Cheever, who handled such serious political topics, wrote with great energy and ability; and Mrs. Stowe's letters in the same troubled times, however pleasant, lost fire in comparison with his excellent editorials.

The suspension of her serial story marred her relationship with the *Independent.* In announcing her inability to continue on April 4, 1861, she came the nearest to a direct falsehood of her career, for she gave as a reason the necessity of revisiting Maine for further observation "to give the story the finish and completeness I wish." For this white lie she made full atonement in "A Card" of November 21, 1861, announcing the resumption of the story in the following issue. Here she again fibbed a bit by asking "Who could write on stories, that had a son to send to battle?" Finally, however, she gave the true reason for her suspension of writing—overwork.

Mr. Theodore Tilton, her explanation showed, had wheedled her into promising a serial, although she was already committed internationally to the *Atlantic* and to *Cornhill* for *Agnes of Sorrento.* Overpowered by Tilton's immense personal charm, she had promised more than she could fulfill. The *Atlantic* and *Cornhill* came first, and the *Independent* as soon as she could find time for it. The delay did no good to *The Pearl of Orr's Island*—it is the explanation of the often noted discrepancy between the two halves of the story—but it taught her that there were limits to her strength and creative ability. She was never caught again, except for an occasional week's delay from illness, and she resumed her character of utter dependability and commercial honor.

One special service that the *Independent* performed for Mrs. Stowe was to act as her press agent. Her name on its front page week after week, whether she was writing for the issue or not, had the effect of a reiterated advertisement; and beyond this the magazine generously reviewed her books. When *The Minister's Wooing* was attacked, the *Independent* used an editorial "Theology and Morality in the Minister's Wooing," admitting that she had made errors but denying that she had gone to Unitarianism. On the same page it printed another article on the same subject, as well as a letter from a correspondent on another page (February 9, 1860).

Today one would assume logrolling, but members of Mrs. Stowe's circle never suspected themselves guilty of such a vicious practice. When Catherine, many years previously, had written to Mrs. Sigourney that she wanted to increase her influence, she had meant that she wanted more and bigger markets for her essays. "To make myself known, and as popular as I can, with all classes of readers" (Harveson, 77), would mean, to a modern commercial writer, to find the most profitable mass markets; but to Catherine, and to all the Beechers, it meant "increasing the sphere of influence." Thus the *Independent*, and later the *Christian Union*, labored successfully to increase Mrs. Stowe's sphere of influence.

III   Hearth and Home

When the weekly domestic magazine *Hearth and Home* was established, beginning with the issue of December 26, 1868, the editors were Donald G. Mitchell and Harriet Beecher Stowe. This was the first and the last time in her career that Mrs. Stowe took public responsibility for preparing a magazine regularly. Her duties, slighter than her title of associate editor suggested, were limited to supplying a weekly column; for Mitchell shouldered the main labors. Even this routine work was beyond her, for her last column appeared on October 30, 1869, and her name disappeared from the editorial acknowledgments on November 20, 1869. She broke off her relationship with the magazine for the best of reasons: she was not receiving her pay. Even with money, the strain of regular weekly assignments might have been too much for her, although she cannot be accused of laziness, since in the years 1868-69 four of her books were published: *The Chimney-Corner, Men of Our Times, Oldtown Folks,* and *The American Woman's Home.*

Busy as she kept herself, Mrs. Stowe was always a trifle temperamental, as well as subject to fits of illness. That she missed only four issues before her resignation is remarkable, but the contributions themselves show, in their skipping from topic to topic and their occasional emptiness, what her difficulties were. Since none of her forty papers for *Hearth and Home* has been reprinted, a glance at them, in their original order, is a rewarding glimpse into her workshop.

The first issue contained her "Greeting," one of her clearest statements on the position of women. With the liberals she maintained that women should have the right to vote, to engage in business, or to make themselves useful as they wished; but with the conservatives she maintained also that the rights of voting and trading were far inferior to woman's greatest vocation, that of wife and mother. Thus she offered a benevolent if distant encouragement to the movement for feminine freedom, but left herself free to oppose any particular step taken on its behalf.

For the next three months she switched from topic to topic as if searching for a theme. She wrote on "How to Treat Babies" and "Rights of Dumb Animals"; she discussed gardening, beautiful chromo-lithographs, and commercial writing; and she explained how to buy a carpet—as in Christopher Crowfield's "The Ravages of a Carpet"—and how to beautify living rooms with flower pots made from tin cans. She also took a week's vacation.

In April her column was acceptably filled with travel letters from Florida. These are in the spirit of the later book, *Palmetto-Leaves*, her never-ending enthusiasm establishing her as one of the best publicity agents Florida was ever to have. The May articles were also entirely on her travels, which were summed up in her first two June articles, "From the St. John's South, to the St. John's, North," and "Homeward from Canada."

For the last weeks of June she discussed, in two installments, "What Shall Young Girls Read?" In the first of these she recommended the *Pictorial History of England* and *Ivanhoe*. The second went on to *The Talisman*, Miss Strickland's *Queens of England*, and the histories of Froude and Macaulay.

On July 3 she printed a sympathetic and informative article on "The Colored Labor of the South," an evaluation of progress since emancipation. After this took another week's leave, and followed it on July 17 with a pointless discussion of "Country and City."

Beginning on July 24, 1869, the magazine provided her with illustrated covers depicting, week by week, "Four Scenes in the

Life of a Country Boy," really choice period pieces upon which she commented appropriately. The titles, "Leaving Home," "The Temptation and the Fall," "Further On," and "At Last," practically tell the story. The pitiful yokel, having become a forger, is led off to prison by a detective—the climax of a series of scenes not quite in the spirit of Hogarth.

On August 21, 1869, she discussed "The Handy Man" around the house, and the following week returned, more vitally, to women's rights in "What is and What is not the Point in the Woman Question." In a word, the point is money; and justice still holds, as in Revolutionary days, that taxation without representation is tyranny. Another week's leave of absence followed.

September found the associate editor on her travels again, and four articles, starting September 11, 1869, were inspired by various places in New England. On October 9, 1869, she changed the subject to ask, "Who Earned that Money?" answering that the wife, by saving, was also a true earner. The article for October 16, 1869, considered "Our Early Rose Potatoes," and that for October 30, called simply "Hartford," told the world that she was home.

Once there, she lacked either ambition or energy to continue further with the insolvent *Hearth and Home*. The Byron controversy was already upon her, and she was saving her energies for the publication, within the years 1870-71, of *Lady Byron Vindicated, Little Pussy Willow, My Wife and I,* and *Pink and White Tyranny.*

Mrs. Stowe's associate editorship of *Hearth and Home,* though merely an episode in her busy life, shows her difficulties in finding vital subjects for weekly discourses. She had the habit of repeating herself and the equally fatal one of using up her good leads too fast. When in doubt, she fell back upon her old standbys, except that straight religious discourse was not permitted in *Hearth and Home.* Travel became her greatest source of copy: fourteen of her forty articles are about travel, eight of them concerning Florida. Six of the others are on homemaking problems (the special field covered by the magazine), three on feminism, one on kindness to animals, and eight on miscellaneous subjects. The only new vein uncovered is a group of seven articles on writing and reading, a significant addition to her meager comments on these subjects in her letters and the collected *Writings*.

In her own manner of writing, no distinctions appear between these *Hearth and Home* articles and the earlier ones for the *Independent*—or even the later ones for the *Christian Union*. They are hasty sketches, far removed from the more carefully edited longer essays for the *Atlantic Monthly*.

IV   The Christian Union

Of all the journalistic connections of the Beechers, *The Christian Union* was probably the happiest personally. This magazine—which later developed into the *Outlook*, enjoying a long and successful existence—was published by the firm of John Bruce Ford and Company, the principal publisher of Mrs. Stowe's later books.

The firm itself was established out of love for Henry Ward Beecher. Both Mr. Ford and his younger partner, John Raymond Howard, who has told the story in his *Remembrance of Things Past* (New York, 1925), were idolizers at the Beecher shrine, and the firm was founded to exploit their idol's talents. As Howard tells the story, the first act of Ford and Company was to advance Beecher ten thousand dollars for a life of Christ (215-18). While waiting for the manuscript, which was long delayed, it occupied itself profitably in publishing such successful books as Horace Greeley's *Recollections of a Busy Life*, and *The Trotting Horse in America*, by two experts on that exciting subject. Soon followed weekly reprints of Beecher's sermons, later a regular feature of the *Christian Union* itself.

All was optimism around Ford and Company's offices, for the firm was prosperous from the start, and when the *Christian Union* was finally reorganized in 1870, with Beecher himself as editor, its pages breathed a calm assurance that all was well with the world. Failure was to come almost as suddenly a few years later with Beecher's spectacular fall from public favor, but meanwhile there was a profitable subscription list of over two hundred thousand names (Howard, 306).

In his "Salutory" for the new magazine, dated January 1, 1870, Beecher explained the title and policy of the paper. It was to be a family journal; that is, of general, not specifically religious interest, but still of "distinctly Christian influence." It was to be devoted to "oneness of Christian sympathy," though not to "oneness of Church . . . that phantom, a Universal Corporate Unity of Christians." Beecher was determined to avoid all doctrinal controversy in an attempt to shed his own views upon as wide a segment of the magazine-buying public as possible. He worked energetically on the *Christian Union,* supplying weekly chats and editorials as well as his sermons; and, even during the days of the Tilton trial, he kept a brave face in talking of himself and his troubles.

In the second issue he began introducing the members of his family to the magazine's clientele. Catherine was first, with an article against woman suffrage that stirred up controversy for some time. She also announced a campaign for funds to establish a woman's university, emphasizing a strong department of domestic science, with herself and Mrs. Stowe as president and associate president. Shortly afterward the magazine, as if by an afterthought, began advertising a book on domestic science written by the same two ladies.

On May 7, 1870, Calvin Stowe began contributing articles on the New Testament, a series which later broadened its scope and became one of the regular features. In the same issue Mrs. Stowe also appeared with "Who Ought to Come to Florida?"—her familiar type of press-agentry for the delightful South which her regular readers had encountered before. Meanwhile Mrs. Henry Ward Beecher had already opened her department on "The Household," and she was followed, from time to time, by Thomas K. and all other Beechers who cared to write for publication.

In this happy family gathering, Mrs. Stowe seems to have felt as thoroughly at home as Henry Ward himself. For his magazine she wrote three serial novels, *My Wife and I, We and Our Neighbors,* and *Poganuc People;* three series of shorter articles that became *Woman in Sacred History, Footsteps of the Master,* and *Palmetto-Leaves;* a good share of *Sam Lawson's Oldtown Fireside Stories,* as well as a large number of miscellaneous articles, over fifty of which were never reprinted. From 1870 to her retirement, the *Christian Union* received most of her attention, and happy association with it reflects or perhaps accounts for the mellowness of her later works.

A few of her miscellaneous unreprinted articles lie outside her usual topics. Two which belong in this category have the title "The Indians of St. Augustine" (April 18 and 25, 1877), a lively account of the education of Indians lately brought to Florida from the West.

On subjects not entirely new, yet not entirely old, one of the most successful was an obituary notice on Horace Greeley, mixing praise and reservation which was much more personal than the stereotyped account in *Men of Our Times.* Other obituary notices give evidence of the passing of the years.

Spiritualism continued to disturb her. Four articles from September 3 to October 1, 1879, dealt with this subject, and she reached the conclusion that Christianity is more essential to salvation than spiritualism but that, if departed spirits seek to make us Christian, they may possibly be genuine. This idea was repeated a month later; but a review of Robert Dale Owen's *The Debatable Land,* January 24, 1872, took a negative viewpoint; it rejected spiritualism firmly in favor of Bible revelation.

The familiar lay sermons continued. "Our Lord's Bible," July 13, 1870, urges Christians to study the basic book of their faith. "The Traveler's Talisman," August 20, 1870, praises faith and prayer. "Transplanting—a Parable," August 21, 1872, repeats her idea of earthly sorrow as heavenly discipline. "I believe in the Resurrection of the Body," October 30, 1872, re-expresses that article of her faith. "Does God Answer Prayer?" November 13, 1872, is only one of her several assurances that He does. "A Heroic Squash," three years later, is a parable to show "the power of moral endurance."

It is unnecessary to continue the catalogue. Mrs. Stowe kept her activity and her old interests to the end. She still wrote her travel sketches from North or South, and she still waxed enthusiastic over chromo-lithographs such as those given by the *Christian Union* as premiums with subscriptions: she was convinced they could "hardly be distinguished from the originals." She showed herself to be a kindly, alert old lady who was greatly concerned with parents who failed to teach their children not to put "Pins in Pussy's Toes" and who was encouraged by the superior morality shown by the Earl of Beaconsfield in *Lothair* —which she thought, in its improvement over *Vivian Grey,* to be a clear indication of the improved moral standards of British society generally.

She continued to write a little about the Negroes and a little about prohibition, but without rancor. She was inclined to take a hopeful view of the world. As she said, in the last letter to the *Christian Union* from Florida (Feburary 7, 1877): "We are as quiet as a mill-pond. . . . Come down, ye weary, heavy-laden . . . where everybody is good-natured!"

Such was the ending of her literary career. The sweet and gentle *Our Folks at Poganuc*, as it was called in the magazine, ran from November 28, 1877, to June 12, 1878; and her name was not included among the prospective contributors for 1879.

V *Other Magazines*

Of all the magazines for which Mrs. Stowe wrote regularly, the *Atlantic Monthly* got from her the best work, very likely because it demanded the best. However that may be, when Houghton Mifflin and Company published her *Writings* in 1896, the editors salvaged every scrap from the *Atlantic,* from the "Mourning-Veil" of the first issue to the explosive "True Story of Lady Byron" and the subsequent *Fireside Stories.* Unfortunately the anonymous editors of the *Writings* were not industrious in searching the files of magazines besides their own, so that any important impressions to be gained from them can still be gathered only from the original files.

But there can be no question that, on the whole, Mrs. Stowe's *Atlantic* work is a fair sample of her best efforts. The magazine was so much less provincial than the *Evangelist*, the *Watchman and Reflector, Hearth and Home,* or the *Christian Union,* that what she wrote for it is best adapted, on the whole, to give a favorable impression—though not a complete or even an adequate impression—of her work. The *Atlantic* took itself seriously as a mouthpiece for American culture and consequently demanded good style as well as good sense. Lowell, Howells, and other editors who worked over manuscripts conscientiously, prepared them for an eternity within covers as well as for a month on the parlor table.

Of the other magazines which bought her output, Edward Everett Hale's *Old and New* likewise had serious aims, but it lasted only four years. A curious mixture of the scholarly and the simple, it combined erudite articles on American political literature or Chinese transcendentalism with Mrs. Stowe's own childish *Pink and White Tyranny.*[1]

Albion W. Tourgee's *Our Continent,* which was also both interesting and short-lived, was a popular literary magazine with special emphasis on the South. To it Mrs. Stowe made a single contribution, "The Captain's Story," in which she tried her hand at Southern local color. *The Revolution*—not so inflammatory as it might seem from the title—was also a lively little publication for woman's rights conducted by Elizabeth Cady Stanton and Susan B. Anthony. Although it announced Mrs. Stowe among its contributors, it ran protests against her conservatism as well as minor contributions from her pen. Other contacts, such as that with the important *North American Review,* for which she wrote a single article, are likewise too slight to be of ascertainable significance.

All in all, however, the story of her association with magazines, covering a half century from 1833 to 1882, is the most revealing story of her literary life. Magazines were not only her daily sustenance; they were also the only literary school she ever attended. They may have led her from the path of true artistry, but they made her the figure she became. Without their constant repetition of her name in their tables of contents and their editorial discussions she could not have been *the* Mrs. Stowe that everybody came to know and most people to admire. Never their hack, in the sense of a conscienceless purveyor of whatever was wanted, she was nonetheless their creature.

CHAPTER 8

Artistry

A DISCUSSION of Mrs. Stowe purely as literary artist would be brief. One can consider her ideas, her prejudices, her emotions, her hidden depths, all of which find their way into her writings; but of conscious art there exists barely the microscopic drop indispensable for clinical analysis. Her passion for writing, obvious in early girlhood,[1] led her to much soul-searching about what to say, but to few questions about how to say it well.

Why such indifference, with the examples of Poe and Hawthorne before her in her younger days? We have only hints—not so much an answer to the question as a review of neglected opportunities. As George Sand said of her, Mrs. Stowe was certainly a saint, but she was perhaps not a man of letters. It is doubtful that any writer of comparable reputation has been less concerned than she with the art or craft of writing. The box-office was her most trusted teacher, critic, and literary conscience.

In her vocabulary "fiction" was a repugnant word, with insinuations of frivolity and indecency. "The propensity of the human mind to fiction," she wrote in the preface to an omnibus collection, *A Library of Famous Fiction,* "is one of those irrepressible forces against which it has always proved vain to contend."[2] The thought saddened her, and she recollected that in her youth a favorite subject for written compositions in the schools had been "On the Disadvantages of Novel-reading." "Since the world must read fiction," she continued, "let us have the best in an attractive household form"; that is, in a bowdlerized version where, vain as fiction might be, it could at least avoid vulgarity. "Swift's genius commands our admiration," she confessed, "but his words should never be introduced into the home-circle save in such revised and cleanly editions as the present one" (p. x).

As editor, as well as writer, she found a duty in restraining the shallow people from worse than folly. *A Library of Famous Fiction*, a conglomeration dictated by publishing expediency, contained, with its merely trivial, commercially desirable tales, that gem of gems and perhaps the only story of which she unreservedly approved, *Pilgrim's Progress*.[3] In childhood she had known its terrors; in womanhood, had found its joys. Was it not the story of her own life? But by most readers of fiction, she knew, Bunyan's or her own high morality was unattainable. The worldliness of the reading public was one of the Disadvantages of Novel-writing.

I *Lady Byron Vindicated* (1870)

Mrs. Stowe was not endowed with an avid appetite for literary subtleties. One of the reasons that she wrote carelessly was that she read carelessly. About the bulk of her reading there was nothing meager, no more than about the bulk of her writing; but only one writer of mere literature moved her deeply, and she pursued his memory with savage vindictiveness.

Lord Byron, that glamorous rascal who fascinated moralists and young girls in the early nineteenth century, has the honor of being the only author to whom Mrs. Stowe devoted a book; and the title, *Lady Byron Vindicated* (1870), placed the emphasis on the poet's wife. In the two of them Mrs. Stowe found echoes of herself: Byron, a kindred imagination tempted by the Devil; and Lady Byron, a kindred conscience speaking for the Lord. The book itself, an accidental outgrowth of an indignant article for the *Atlantic Monthly*, was the offspring of a fascinated horror at the poet's sinfulness and of affection for his wife.[4]

Mrs. Stowe's writings about Byron illustrate many conflicts. In her own mind, she was protecting the memory of a noble wife against the sneers and insults of lewd females and dishonorable males; but, to outsiders unconversant with such high morality, she was gratuitously attacking Byron, Moore, Mrs. Leigh, Christopher North, the Countess Guiciolli, and the whole manhood of Great Britain. Her excitability (coupled with resultant errors of interpretation) made her recital of essential truth sound like lurid falsehood. Both the original *Atlantic* article and her later expansion exhibited nearly to perfection—in spite of assistance from hired legal and historical consultants—the knack of being unconvincing. Dickens was only one of those who privately wished her in the pillory, just as the anonymous pamphleteer "Outis" was only one of those who publicly consigned her to the lunatic asylum.

How unjust her opponents were, her own conscience duly advised her. In Lady Byron's words, "Mrs. Stowe, he was guilty of incest with his own sister!" Vainly might she quote this assertion, and vainly repeat the answer which she had intended as reassuring: "My dear friend, I have heard that." Long before reaching this point in her narrative, she had lost her case through frantic argumentation and vituperation. The sordid details, instead of substantiating her claims, more deeply prejudiced her readers against her. In the controversy that followed, the reliability of her facts was less debated than the incredibility of her character.[5] When Bayard Taylor asked his friend E. C. Stedman what he thought of *Lady Byron Vindicated*, Stedman replied that Lady Byron was "a jealous virtuous prude" and Mrs. Stowe "a gossiping green old granny."[6]

Ignoring ugly interpretations that would be put upon her motives, Mrs. Stowe gave free reign to her pride in having associated with the British nobility—bestrewing her pages prodigally with "noble lords" and "ladies of rank"—while at the same time she charged a gigantic conspiracy in which half the literary men of England had consciously and persistently blackened Lady Byron's reputation over a period of fifty years. To these absurdities she added, with surpassing literary maladroitness, an alluring portrait of Byron as a glamorous victim of "moral insanity" (374) and a repellent picture of Lady Byron as an inhumanly faultless wife.

To a mere outsider incapable of appreciating such unselfish service, *Lady Byron Vindicated* reads as though the writing of it was an exhilarating double excursion into high society and into an exciting moral underworld, the soul of Lord Byron. The more of his work she read, the more clearly Mrs. Stowe understood the cause of his unutterable wickedness. She ascribed his downfall to the gloom of Calvinism from which he had suffered in his youth. Byron fell, she rose; their common struggle, a deep bond of sympathy, made them spiritual lovers.

In a woman nearing sixty, the adolescent excitement of *Lady Byron Vindicated* is amazing: it was the exasperated outgrowth of a lifelong crush. When she had first read one of his poems— it was "The Corsair," and she was thirteen at the time—she was, as she has said, astonished and electrified; and when she heard that Byron was dead, she prayed and wept as though the world were coming to an end. She was thrilled when, the next Sunday, her father preached a funeral sermon for the dead bard, lamenting his wasted powers. Nor did the memory of Byron fade; for she recalled that her father often said, in his evangelical fervor, that he wished he might have talked to Byron, to straighten the fellow out and make him a harpist for Christ (AF, 38-39).

Harriet herself, at this early age, started a play in blank verse, *Cleon* by name, in which the hero is a dissolute but basically noble youth of the Emperor Nero's court—"the prime companion of our revels," as Nero says. Converted to Christianity, the hero appears to be headed toward martyrdom. As the play was not completed, the fate of the Byronic hero, whether Christian martyrdom or Christian marriage, remains undisclosed.[7]

During her formative years in Cincinnati, Byron was almost as important a subject for the local newspapers as the cholera epidemics. Not only did frequent short notices appear about his works, but the *Chronicle* on one occasion (November 3, 1832) devoted the entire front page to reprinting a critical article from a London review. Throughout the first half of her life, Mrs. Stowe was continually reminded of what a great, bad man Byron had been. Her colleague Whittier, writing in the *National Era* (July 15, 1847), stated that "in Byron we see Power, uncontrolled by Principle, Genius divorced from Goodness." This was not only the same moral estimate of the poet as James Hall's in the *Western Monthly Magazine,* but the same as her father's in his obituary sermon. Forty-five years after Byron's death Mrs. Stowe was also, in her far from delicate way, straightening the fellow out.

In preparation for her *Atlantic* article, Oliver Wendell Holmes, somewhat against his judgment, gave Mrs. Stowe his "literary counsel and supervision." To his friend John Motley he wrote, on July 18, 1869, that the most interesting news he could impart concerned the forthcoming September *Atlantic*. He predicted, soundly enough, that it would startle the world. "I was not consulted about the matter of publishing Lady Byron's revelations. Mrs. Stowe assured me that she had made up her mind about *that*."[8] Argument, he had learned from experience, was wasted upon such determination. One questions whether she profited from the limited criticism she allowed him; for the writing, although not so slipshod in the article as in the expanded version of the book, was hysterical and unconvincing.

Henry Adams, one should recall, considered it the best work she had done up to that time, ranking it for effectiveness even above the Topsy scenes of *Uncle Tom's Cabin*. His statement, however, dates from October, 1869, when the excitement was reaching its height; and, as the full passage in his letter demonstrates, he was not overcome with admiration for any of her work.[9] His praise was comparative, not absolute. The furor of the moment forgotten, Mrs. Stowe's entire contribution to the Byron legend is revelatory primarily of an abiding juvenile fascination for an abominable gay young devil.

II *Favorite Writers from the Past*

Less spectacular in its effects than Byronism, but pervasive in the long run, was the influence upon Mrs. Stowe of another romanticist and liberal, Mme. de Staël, whose romance *Corinne; or, Italy* she discovered independently in 1833. That this novel, an international best-seller, should have found its way to Cincinnati and into the Beecher household was less remarkable than that it should have awakened such impassioned thought in Harriet Beecher as her letters from the period show. *Corinne: or, Italy* may appear to modern readers either a high-flown demonstration that true love is not smooth or a diluted guide-book to southern Europe, both of which, considered unhistorically, it is: but to Harriet Beecher, in her early twenties, it was a storehouse of wisdom and an ideal of personal perfection.

Byron paid *Corinne* the compliment of describing it as more dangerous to virtue than any of his writings, more insidious because it disguised vice under a pious aspiration. It was the veneer that attracted young Harriet. Earnestly as she might regret the heroine's inconstancy of heart and her lack of steadfast patriotism, there was much more to arouse her enthusiasm despite "the difference of their countries and creeds."

Above all else, the character of the heroine was filled with alluring possibilities. Beautiful, talented, rich, Corinne possessed the passion of Juliet and the dignity of a vestal virgin. Divine inspiration was enthroned in her eyes, and her talents were so extraordinary that normal rules for judging women failed to apply to her. Like Harriet, Corinne appreciated everything that was grand and noble, hated the selfishness of the human race, longed fiercely to be loved, and suffered wretchedness in her prison of small-town life, harried by untoward climate and by anxiety. Both women had known the loss in childhood of their mothers, and both had endured melancholy girlhoods under the care of stepmothers.

At the crucial moment of first reading in 1833, Harriet found immediate comfort in the aphorisms liberally sprinkled through the book—"The Impassioned are far more liable to weakness than the fickle"—and hope in the question, "Ought not every woman, like every man, to follow the bent of her own talents?" For years the image of Corinne kept reappearing before her: the inspired prophetess raised by purely feminine traits above the blurred half-virtue of a male world. An Americanized Corinne, maternal and matured, remained an ideal for womanhood.

Less complicated than her attraction to either Byron or Mme. de Staël was Mrs. Stowe's admiration for Sir Walter Scott, her favorite poet, whose *Lay of the Last Minstrel* she could—and did—recite complete from memory. Nor was her devotion to Scott limited to his poetry. When she was a girl, her father had excepted Scott's prose stories from his general condemnation of novels as trash, and in one summer the family had read *Ivanhoe* seven times. This childhood pleasure in the Waverley novels she renewed with her own children, at one time (1850) reading them all in historical sequence to enliven the routine of history lessons.[10]

The first poetry she had ever read was Scott's ballads, which impressed her much more than Burns's poems, to which she was soon introduced. She liked to contrast Scott with Byron in order to praise the former for his higher morality. "He never makes young ladies feel that they would like to marry corsairs, pirates, or sentimental villains of any description," she wrote in *Sunny Memories* (I, 143). This judgment she repeated in a later essay for children, "Sir Walter Scott and his Dogs," in which he is mentioned as "one of the greatest geniuses of the world," and Byron as "the great rival poet to Scott. . . . not so good or so wise a man by many degrees, but very celebrated in his day."[11] She loved Scott wholeheartedly and was immeasurably fonder of his work than of Shakespeare's.

"Shakespeare, Madam, is obscene," a Cincinnati *litterateur* had declared to Mrs. Trollope, "and thank God, we are sufficiently advanced to have found it out." Mrs. Stowe's visit to Stratford was the duty call demanded by a great reputation; for like her fellow-townsman, she suspected Shakespeare's obscenity. Although professing the conventional admiration for him, she squirmed under the coarseness of his plays; she doubted the accuracy of his history; and she looked disapprovingly upon his frivolity. On the whole, she was repelled most by the "weirdness" of his writing. She feared that he lacked a progressive mind for enthusiastic reform, and she softened to him only when thinking of Queen Elizabeth, "this most repulsive and disagreeable woman," the "belligerent old Gorgon" whose gross taste had disgraced her entire court and period.[12] *The Tempest* was an exception, for she quoted approvingly from it in *The Minister's Wooing*, in *The Pearl of Orr's Island* and in "A Student's Sea Story," from *Sam Lawson's Oldtown Fireside Stories*. The attractions of *The Tempest* were the innocence of Miranda and the beauty of the lyric "Full fathom five."

Like Shakespeare, Milton—an old favorite of her father—failed to impress her deeply. In *Sunny Memories* she called him "cold" (I, 207; II, 2, 279), and apparently preferred Dr. Watts, "a born poet" (II, 27). Lyman's sympathies seemed to have been with Satan, whom Harriet found a less persuasive tempter than Lord Byron. Although Milton is referred to in *Uncle Tom's Cabin* and in *The Minister's Wooing,* he is prominently mentioned only in *Oldtown Folks* (268, 422, 433, 435, 442 447, 477, 501, 604). In it he becomes a definite symbol of Puritanism, comparable in significance to the New England divines, Bellamy, Edwards, Eliot, and Hopkins.

A list of all Mrs. Stowe's casual literary references would be long, for her reading was not deficient in quantity, however superficial her responses seem to have been.[13] At thirteen she was studying Latin, French, and Italian, and a few years later she was translating Ovid and teaching Virgil. Even in earlier childhood, as her brother wrote to her aunt, Harriet read everything she could "lay hands on." The habit of rapid reading persisted throughout her life, in the same spirit of childhood enthusiasm.

She obviously admired Samuel Richardson more than casually (though she never suggested that his psychological subtlety appealed to her), and had been willing to skip a dinner invitation to plunge once more into the enchanting pages of *Sir Charles Grandison.* She mentions this book in *The Minister's Wooing* as inevitable in the library of the well-taught young woman of the late eighteenth century, along with the *Spectator, Robinson Crusoe,* the Bible, and the writings of Jonathan Edwards.[14] Miss Edgeworth was another permanent favorite, both for her novels and for her tales for children. It was only at maturity that she dipped into Chaucer: "I read Chaucer a great deal yesterday, and am charmed at the reverential Christian spirit in which he viewed all things."[15]

III   *Contemporaries*

If Mrs. Stowe's taste for the great writers of the past was conventional in its limitations, her taste for her contemporaries was no less so. She was surprised during her first visit in England at the respect she found for Emerson, Hawthorne, and Prescott, none of whom she had discovered herself. Hawthorne she at first viewed with skepticism, and it was only after overcoming her distrust of his strange viewpoint that she could unqualifiedly endorse him after his death as a "wonderful fellow" and "our most exquisite writer."[16] One doubts that she ever reconciled herself to Emerson, her father's early feuds with the Unitarians predisposing her against anything which smacked of transcendentalism.

For Holmes and Whittier, on the other hand, she had from the first personal and hence literary liking. They had both been associated with the *Atlantic* from its earliest days, and Whittier had also been a contributing editor to the *National Era* and to the *Independent*. With the good Doctor she carried on an extended and vivacious exchange of letters, over thirty pages of which, on his side, can be found in the memoir of his life. He praised her work, but no more highly than he did that of Elizabeth Stuart Phelps; he discussed religion with her, no more seriously than with his obscure fundamentalist correspondents; he compared himself, modestly, with her. Her letters always touched him, he declared; and his frank and personal answers are evidence that he enjoyed answering them.

Mrs. Stowe was also greatly attached to Mrs. Browning, whom she met in Italy; what she thought of Robert, or he of her, remains a matter for surmise. In later years she came to know George Eliot, who seems to have been indulgently amused by both the authoress and her Rabbi husband, although somewhat puzzled when Harriet insisted that the pedant Casaubon in *Middlemarch* was drawn from Mr. Lewes. Nor would "G. Elliot" (as Mrs. Stowe referred to her in a letter to Mr. Fields) have been entirely pleased at another compliment paid her by Mrs. Stowe. "A Dog's Mission," one of Harriet's moral tales for children, is by imitation a tribute to *Silas Marner*. In this parable a hardhearted old maid, Zarviah Avery by name, is restored to natural sympathy by the intrusion into her life of a stray dog. Gradually her circle of tolerance extends from dogs to children; and at the end of the tale she is reconciled to her brother (whom she had driven out of her house to California in his childhood) and, like Silas Marner, to the entire human race.[17]

Among the prominent literary men of her time, Lowell was the most important to her. As editor of the *Atlantic,* he was able to adopt the tone of personal interest that she esteemed so highly. His love of the old New England was as strong as hers; and the "famous" Puritan conscience was, as Henry James pointed out in his judicious obituary notice, an integral part of Lowell's nature. Best of all, he praised her work extravagantly.

The Minister's Wooing was, according to his words (or at least according to the impression he tried to give through them), an imperishable masterpiece.[18] Whittier was much sounder in saying of the story to Lowell that it opened with promise, but that it was thin, lacking the fullness of detail necessary to let the reader know in what part of the world he was supposed to find himself, in what age, and in what climate.[19]

If contemporary writers were not a chief influence upon Mrs. Stowe's work, there was also a perceptible shade of condescension in their attitude towards her. She was in the New England group without really being accepted by it, a rejection partly the result of her sex and partly of her principles. How she was denied their full confidence is indicated in a letter Charles Eliot Norton wrote Arthur Hugh Clough about the forthcoming new magazine, the *Atlantic*. After naming Motley, Holmes, Emerson, and Lowell as contributors, Norton mentioned the projected policy of printing most articles anonymously, using authors' names only when the names were worth more than the articles. The first issue, he said, would contain two such articles: one of them was to be Mrs. Stowe's.[20]

A more spectacular example of the distinction the eminent gentlemen drew between themselves and Mrs. Stowe is afforded by the records of an *Atlantic* dinner of 1859, to which, after considerable trepidation, the women contributors had been invited. Only two ladies appeared, Miss Harriet Prescott and Mrs. Stowe, who had accepted on condition that no wine was to be served. As Lowell wrote to Emerson, this proviso tied a witches-knot; and the manner in which the gentlemen hoodwinked the prohibitionist by serving themselves wine in water glasses has been told with richly genteel humor by Thomas Wentworth Higginson, one of the unregenerate participants in the ruse.

After a cold, wineless start, the party livened a bit, as Lowell assured Mrs. Stowe that *Tom Jones* was the best novel ever written and Holmes tried to convince Professor Stowe that profanity had originated in the free use of language in the pulpit. Both of the Stowes were heard to observe later that they had been disappointed in the dinner; for, while the company was undoubtedly distinguished, "the conversation was not quite what they had been led to expect."[21]

Professional envy was a vicious trait completely alien to Mrs. Stowe's character. She was invariably kindly and generous toward young writers (except French novelists whom she never named) and humanitarian reformers. Books for which she wrote introductory notes reveal her tastes: *An Inside View of Slavery*, by C. G. Parsons (1855); the *Works of Charlotte Elizabeth Tonna* (1844-45); *Tell it All; the Story of a Life's Experiences in Mormonism*, by Mrs. T. B. H. Stenhouse (1874); *The Incarnation; or, Pictures of the Virgin and her Son*, by Charles Beecher (1849). She occasionally reviewed or discussed in her magazine departments, books on spiritualism and theology, and she thought well enough of Mrs. A. D. T. Whitney, the author of *Faith Gartney's Girlhood* (1863) and other books for girls, to write a biographical sketch for an omnibus volume called *Our Famous Women* (1884) in which she also published a sketch of her sister Catherine.

In her later years, although she liked *The Luck of Roaring Camp* volume by Bret Harte and praised the local-color sketches of George Washington Cable,[22] she was more gushingly enthusiastic about fiction with a stronger evangelical appeal. Among lesser-known novels, she was carried away by a certain *What Answer?* (1868) by Anna Dickinson, a woman of varied talents, mostly of a performing sort, among which writing fiction was not included. This novel, dealing with the social effects of miscegenation, was greeted by Mrs. Stowe as "a noble deed," to the great disgust of the New York *Nation*, which responded that *What Answer?* was "emphatically a bad novel—without interest, even possessing some positive qualities which inflict pain on any one who in the least values art." This was a criticism which Mrs. Stowe had already discounted: "Works of art be hanged! You had a braver thought than that." Despite such endorsements by Mrs. Stowe and Lydia Maria Child, the "noble deed" failed. What remained was Mrs. Stowe's encouragement: "Your poor old grandma in this work rejoices to find it in your brave young hands."[23]

Still another reforming novel that she praised with possibly excessive enthusiasm was *Environment; a Story of Modern Society*, by her biographer, Florine Thayer McCray. "It is truly a *Christian* story," she wrote, July 27, 1887. "The alcohol which wrought all the mischief and danger was prescribed and *insisted on* by a doctor!" The italics are Mrs. Stowe's: "I *must* express the hope that your book will be widely and *thoughtfully* read and do the good it was evidently intended to do."[24]

IV   *Limitations of Craftsmanship*

That *Uncle Tom's Cabin*, Mrs. Stowe's first novel, should have the strongest construction, as well as the richest content, of any of her novels, shows her uncommon inability to profit from the experience of writing. Nothing exhibits more clearly her limited conception of the art than the seven articles on reading and writing for *Hearth and Home* (1869). Bravely she started in the first of these, "Can I Write?" to give practical advice to beginners. Initial attempts should be on a small scale, she advised, recalling her own introduction to the writing business. Writing to be profitable, must be directed toward a particular magazine or editor. A suitable subject for a young woman would be "How to quiet a fretful baby."

A week later she proceeded to the question, "How Shall I Learn to Write?" First, by having something to say, she decided; second, by practicing expression. Much can be learned from the careful study of Hawthorne's *American Notebooks*. This excellent if somewhat advanced advice was followed by a pertinent view of "Faults of Inexperienced Writers." Here she commented soundly on the vices of indefiniteness, unreasonably big words, and unconscious imitation.

These two articles, a promising introduction, proved to contain the sum total of her rhetorical teaching, for by the following week in "How may I Know that I may Make a Writer?" she could invoke only the commercial test. If you have a genius for writing, she said, people will be glad to pay you. "Writing—Commercially," a month and a half later, restated this view. Writing is worth, she repeated, whatever it will bring. Shrewd as these comments are from the commercial angle that was her natural perspective, the food they offer literary art is skimpy. To say what one thinks editors want and in language that readers understand summarizes her advice.

It is a further indication, and a rather odd one, of her lack of literary susceptibility, that her own writing shows so few formal likenesses to her prime favorites. Unresponsive to Byron's satirical wit or to Scott's admirable objectivity, she reproduced only the former's melodrama and the latter's circumstantiality. Except for *Dred*, where the whole treatment recalls Sir Walter, there are few passages indicative of special appreciation of him. Even the Bible, her favorite book of books, which she knew extremely well and which she referred to and quoted constantly, was not a source of literary inspiration.

As her truest admirers have pointed out, Mrs. Stowe was not adept at writing. "A woman like Mrs. Stowe," Miss Jewett wrote charitably, "cannot bring herself to that cold selfishness of the moment for one's work's sake" (*Letters*, 47). The pioneer unauthorized biographer, Mrs. McCray, aware of the imperfections of her idol's writings, was sorrowfully convinced that, despite their genius, they were not stylistic triumphs. "How marvellous a figure in literary history would Harriet Beecher Stowe have been," she lamented, "could she also have been cited as a model of writing, like Thackeray, Irving, or Lydia Maria Child!" (327). Mrs. Fields points to the same fact without invoking the same hallowed names.

Mrs. Stowe's lifetime of writing led to no sure stylistic improvement over her childhood prize-winning composition on natural morality. Throughout her life she had merely, as she once described her method of work, plunged boldly into the discussion of abstruse subjects. Her editor, James T. Fields, who described her habits as "peculiarly her own," commented in astonishment on her powers of concentration: "She *croons*, so to speak, over her writings, and it makes very little difference to her whether there is a crowd of people about her or whether she is alone during the composition of her books."[25] Elizabeth Cady Stanton, the feminist leader, offers another example of Mrs. Stowe's ability to isolate herself in a world of her own. Calling upon her, Mrs. Stanton found her in her sanctum, writing *Lady Byron Vindicated*, while her sister Catherine, in the same room, was also writing. Without any disturbance, the Beecher women dropped their literary work, while Catherine explained to Mrs. Stanton her objections to woman suffrage.[26]

On the whole, Mrs. Stowe's assertions of trance-like absorption in her work are borne out by the evidence. After it was printed, she revised nothing; before it was printed, she seldom

rewrote for exactness. Her comments on *Oldtown Folks*—her
defense when her publisher was impatiently requesting the
promised copy—are almost unique in her correspondence: "I
am bound by the laws of art," she insisted.

> Instead of rushing on, I have often turned back and written over
> with care, that nothing that I wanted to say might be omitted;
> it has cost me a good deal of labor to elaborate this first part,
> namely, to build my theatre and to introduce my actors. My
> labor has all, however, been given to the literary part.[27]

Such efforts were out of the ordinary. According to her own
testimony, she never bothered to use the elementary tools of
punctuation and grammar correctly,[28] although in her school-
teaching days she had begun to instruct children in rhetoric
and composition before she was twenty years old. She never
tried to master other less elementary tools of expression, being
indifferent to her writing except for the amorphous *good* it
would do. William Dean Howells, recalling his struggles with
her manuscript when he was working on the *Atlantic Monthly*,
wrote with gentle frankness of her carelessness. The combined
labors of the magazine staff were invoked to polish her manuscripts. The under proofreader; the head reader; Howells,
verifying quotations, dates, names; the printer; the head reader
again; Howells once more; and finally the head reader, for
a last revision—these were the intermediaries between an authoi
and the fastidious readers of the *Atlantic*. For Mrs. Stowe's
contributions, he revealed, the text was often "largely rewritten"
on the proof-sheets.[29]

Such time-consuming labors of stylistic refinement were
obviously dispensed with in her other writings which, like *We
and Our Neighbors* or *Pink and White Tyranny*, represent more
faithfully her status as literary craftsman. As in reading books
she approached them like time tables to find out where they
would take her, so she wrote them as marketable commodities,
for what they would get her.[30]

As the result of this attitude towards her works, her comments upon them are singularly unenlightening. "We write only
as we are driven, and never know exactly where we are going
to land," reads a sentence of confession from *The Minister's
Wooing* (27). "When the mind is full of one thing, why go

about to write on another?" she asked, in the only comment on writing in *Palmetto-Leaves* (161). As a fictionist she discovered only one principle about herself: that at certain times she could succeed better than at others. She regarded herself as the lucky recipient of fitful inspiration: "When the spirits will help, I can write," was still her attitude in 1868, after thirty years of literary endeavor (AF, 315). More important perhaps to explain stodgy inequalities in her stories is her conception of them as not primarily stories: they were guidebooks to New England or unwilling dilutions of moralizing into "serials," the shapeless, almost endless monsters that made much of her life a nightmare. At any time she would have preferred to write instructive essays like *Footsteps of the Master* (AF, 372).

In this point of view, it must be granted, there was common sense; for she found it difficult to combine things she wanted to say with an artificially imposed plot that, as likely as not, pointed in some altogether different direction. And so it was wise of her to consider her books from a utilitarian viewpoint. In a letter to a friend about *Men of Our Times* she exclaimed that the book, "hang it!" was almost done (AF, 306). She was fully satisfied with it, having discovered that she could write biographies to order, the lives of model beings to inspire young men and women. If only her books could have accomplished what she wanted, she would have been fully justified in her self-satisfaction. To her, at least, they were not hack writing but Service.

CHAPTER 9

Afterword

MRS. STOWE'S LAST YEARS need no long recounting in a survey of her literary career. Hers was not the ideal old age she had described in "The Mourning-Veil," her contribution to the first issue of the *Atlantic*: "God sometimes gives to good men a guileless and holy second childhood, in which the soul becomes childlike, not childish, and the faculties in full fruit and ripeness are mellow without sign of decay." Though she was surrounded by love and material comfort until her death in 1896, her intellect collapsed years before. At the end, she was merely pathetic. Mark Twain has described her, wandering about Hartford—for after 1884, infirmity, first her husband's then her own, had prevented the annual winter tours to Florida. Sometimes he saw her under the care of an attendant and sometimes sneaking about alone, entering the neighbors' houses, drumming to herself on their pianos or startling them with sudden war-whoops.[1]

Before her complete mental collapse, Mrs. Stowe was enabled, for the first time, to live a restful, unhurried life. Even in Hartford, the scene of her girlhood sufferings in sister Catherine's school, she carried with her the inner peace of her calm isle of Patmos. With no more serial stories to be written for younger generations and no new moral revelations to guide them, she was content to leave to them the work of the world, pridefully quoting from her childhood favorite: "My sword I give to him that shall succeed me in my pilgrimage and my courage and skill to him that can get it." Whatever her reservations may have been, the old crusader, belated discoverer of a Nature that was not Calvinistic, escaped the harsh melancholy which, she recalled, Cotton Mather had attributed to aged New Englanders. She was spared that, and in private communion with her God she relinquished her once militant insistence on the continued progress of humanity. No longer scolding it or improving it with pulpit evangelism, she would calmly view the human race, freed from her immature concern for either its momentary problems or its ultimate destiny.

She was not a new woman, surprising as her transformation appears, for this blessed autumn mood was not entirely the creation of her last years. The privilege of indulging it continually, which was new, was in itself enough to alter her character amazingly. She became purely "home body," purely what Nature had intended and Life so cruelly prevented. Lucy Larcom, who met the older woman in 1862—Mrs. Stowe was then, it will be recalled, barely past fifty—had encountered her in a peaceful moment which presaged the mood of the last years. "It was as beautiful as a page from one of her story books," Miss Larcom noted, referring to the lunch hour. The old stone house at Andover, the golden August day, the thoughtful table arrangements, seen through the hero-worshipping eyes of the yet unrecognized poetess, reached a quiet perfection that remained one of the pleasantest recollections of her life.[2]

A less sentimental observer, William Dean Howells, has also testified to Mrs. Stowe's charm. "Mrs. Stowe was a gracious person," he wrote in reminiscences of his Boston days. He did not know her well, but enough to realize that she was simple, motherly, and "divinely sincere." As he saw her most, before her mental collapse, she was the quiet figure with the "inalienable charm" of her later years.[3]

As an old lady she exhaled continually a modest spiritual dignity far more impressive than the nagging insistence of her younger, active years. "What are queer old women for," Miss Mehitable had asked in *Oldtown Folks*, "if young folks may not have a good laugh out of them now and then?" Had she retained her vigor to the end, she might have been the queer old woman of her foreboding soul; but, as her life turned out, one is less tempted to laugh the older she grows. "I think generally we take ourselves altogether too seriously," Miss Mehitable had offered in explanation of her question (70).

Unlike his wife, the old Professor, as his years advanced, developed a more crotchety disposition and a more grotesque exterior. To Susy Clemens he was Santa Claus: with his portly frame, his lumbering walk, his glorious white bushy whiskers, and his pink little nose—later it withered into a misformed mass—his physical likeness to the children's Christmas friend needed only a red cotton suit to be made perfect. Calvin Stowe was not the careless, absent-minded soul he appeared to observers, for Jonathan Edwards still governed his melancholy thoughts.

His celebrated wife, though she had never been acclaimed a beauty, was a sweet-looking old lady. On her last public appearance she had been the guest at a formal reception arranged by her publishers to honor her seventieth birthday. For this farewell, tributes had been composed by her admirers, among others Whittier and dear Dr. Holmes; and her beloved Henry Ward had come to hear her final comments upon the success of Negro emancipation.

In her private life too she bade the world farewell, sorting through her papers, destroying some and passing the selected remainder on to her son Charles Edward. They would be her biography, and she often hoped that the two of them might manage a collaborative work, which she would call *Pebbles from the Shores of a Past Life,* like the book she and the other children had arranged from her father's last conversations and carefully preserved journals and correspondence. "The desire to leave behind me some recollections of my life, has been cherished by me, for many years past; but failing strength and increasing infirmities"—she was writing from Hartford, September 30, 1889—"have prevented its accomplishment."[4]

In her senility, especially after her return to Hartford in 1884, a kind of wisdom of the sage possessed her. She spoke as one newly inspired by modesty. In the note she composed as a foreword to her son's biography of her, she was still hoping that the book might do good in leading its readers to "a firmer trust in God and a deeper sense of his fatherly goodness"; yet accompanying this old ambition was the new realization of personal inadequacy: "It is perhaps much more accurate as to detail and impression than is possible with any autobiography written late in life." The task, she might have been saying, was gladly resigned by one who had learned its unimportance.

As a legendary abolitionist, either absurd fanatic or heroine of freedom, she took her place in the ranks of American folk characters alongside her Topsy and Eva and Uncle Tom. She will not be dislodged. Whether her books will be read once more, except by antiquarians, is problematical.

In her girlhood Harriet Beecher unquestionably had an adolescent impulse toward creative literature. She read avidly and wrote verse. She had also a bent toward logical analysis, with ability at least equal to that of her brothers. Didacticism and pedagogy were forced upon her, and need for money led her into commercial writing. For about fifteen years she was a modestly successful purveyor of household pap, inherently dissatisfied but not daring to express the open defiance which her miserable existence warranted.

Then came the explosion of *Uncle Tom's Cabin,* a hysterical apocalyptic vision, not a typical or characteristic work but rather an interruption of the normal predictable development of her talent. When she returned to her true subjects, after the *Key* and *Dred,* she had benefited from the prestige of success, the practice of regular publication, and the maturity of five years of independence.

Although Mrs. Stowe was a clever and intelligent woman, she never attained artistic mastery or even a disciplined adequate expression. She had no aesthetic principles and no consistent standards, either for herself or for others. Barrett Wendell was both accurate and kind when he stated (*Literary History of America,* 1901) that she "differed from most American novelists in possessing a spark of genius" or "gleams of creative genius" (355, 366). If she could have been other than she was, "she might have been a figure of lasting literary importance" (355) with "a distinguished place in English fiction" (354). Instead, her stories are rambling and uneven, with only certain "carefully deliberate passages" like the opening chapters of *Oldtown Folks* (with their inestimable debt to Calvin Stowe) "written in a manner which approaches excellence" (355).

For the most part, her flat expression is deadly. Her reflective articles, religious or household journalism, are the record of skirmishes long since won or lost, it matters little which. Her didactic novels and tales are hopelessly outdated. The New England novels, potentially her best work, are reduced to documents of social history by formlessness, the absence of organic design, and arbitrary and artificial plots. The pieces most nearly written for themselves, for fun—such as *Sam Lawson's Oldtown Fireside Stories*—have the monstrous defects of the literary fads of the moment: excessive dialect, pettiness, and the superficiality of anecdotes.

Her recurrent themes were a mixture of the enduringly significant and the banal: the moral superiority of women to men, and how to keep house; Christlike nonaggression, and New England "faculty"; mother-love, and the evil of profanity. On all subjects, great or small, her distinctions between right and wrong were arbitrary and her judgments were pontifical. She could never have understood such a concept as "the fortunate fall." There was none of Emerson's "Brahma" in her universe. The Faust theme—the symbol of a man who could cooperate with the Devil and yet achieve ethical greatness—was alien to her thought. Unlike Emerson, Hawthorne, Melville, or Whitman, she never suspected that sin might also be somehow moral.

Although Mrs. Stowe's writing shows hidden impulses conflicting with these simplified values, it lacks the verbal magic and the complexity of images to keep it alive. A complete reversal of current critical standards will be required to restore her to a position of esteem. Only *Uncle Tom's Cabin*—moving or monstrous—is adequately equipped with symbols, paradoxes, concealed associations, tensions, equivalences, ambiguity, and the paraphernalia of significant expression. More levels of meaning can be observed in a single story like Hawthorne's "Young Goodman Brown" or Poe's "The Fall of the House of Usher" than in an entire novel by Mrs. Stowe.[5] On the documentary level, however, she offers to qualified readers—particularly in *Oldtown Folks*—a wealth of information about our earlier United States and some of the curious kinds of people who were involved in making it what it is.

Notes and References

Preface

1. Ample assurance of Lyman Beecher's intellectual vigor is provided by his *Autobiography*, as edited by his son (New York, 1864). The standard study of Miss Catherine or (note the variant spelling) Catharine Beecher as educator is *Catharine Esther Beecher, Pioneer Educator* (Philadelphia, 1932), by Mae Elizabeth Harveson; appreciation of her leadership in home economics may be found in Kathleen Ann Smallzried, *The Everlasting Pleasure* (New York, 1956), and in James Marston Fitch, *Architecture and the Esthetics of Plenty* (New York, 1961). Perhaps the last sympathetic biography of Henry Ward Beecher is by Lyman Abbott (Boston, 1903). All members of the family receive their approximate due from Lyman Beecher Stowe in *Saints, Sinners and Beechers* (Indianapolis, 1934).

2. The quotations in this paragraph, which are found in several of the biographies, are taken from Annie Fields, ed., *Life and Letters of Harriet Beecher Stowe* (Boston, 1898), pp. 103-6. I have used this book (referred to hereafter as Fields or AF) as a basic reference wherever possible, rather than Forrest Wilson's later vivid and complete biography, *Crusader in Crinoline* (Philadelphia, 1941), because of Mrs. Fields's inherent sympathy with her subject and her infallible sense of nineteenth-century propriety.

3. The most complete version of Lincoln's comment, specifically mentioning "the book," is by Lyman Beecher Stowe, *Saints, Sinners and Beechers,* p. 205. Hawthorne's chagrin is described by Edward Wagenknecht, *Nathaniel Hawthorne, Man and Writer* (New York, 1961), pp. 55, 207.

4. A literary study is no place to decide whether slavery was a fundamental cause of the war, or whether the abolitionist agitation was an aid to emancipation, or even whether Mrs. Stowe's stories were an important influence on either the war or emancipation. Two recent historians of the abolition movement, although they agree on little else, minimize her influence. In Dwight L. Dumond's lavishly illustrated *Antislavery; the Crusade for Freedom in America* (Ann Arbor, 1961), she rates a portrait but is not important enough to receive mention in the index. Louis Filler, *The Crusade against Slavery 1830-1860* (New York, 1960), characterizing *Uncle Tom's*

Cabin as "a major explosion," concludes that its results were "more difficult to gauge" (pp. 208-10). This attitude is very different from the extreme claim of the earlier historian James Ford Rhodes that the book was a major cause of both the war and emancipation, supported with ingenious arguments that have been widely accepted (*History of the United States*, Vol. I, 1893; *Lectures on the American Civil War*, 1913). The current view is much closer to that of Frederick Douglass, who expressed thanks to Mrs. Stowe for her help, as did other Negro leaders who knew her, but rated her service less highly than that of a dozen other women who were more consistent and effective active abolitionists than she. (See his autobiography, first published in 1845 as *Narrative of the Life of Frederick Douglass*, and enlarged and revised several times under different titles; *Life and Times of Frederick Douglass*, [Hartford, 1883], etc.)

5. Tolstoi's praise is in *What is Art*, Heine's in his *Confessions* (*Geständnisse*, written 1853-54). The passage on Uncle Tom is quoted by Israel Tabak, *Heine and his Heritage* (New York, 1956), pp. 200 and 288. Emerson obviously read *Uncle Tom's Cabin* in 1852, for he refers to it in his journal and in several letters (Vol. IV of the 1939 Columbia University Press edition, pp. 302, 303, 311, 319, 343). Macaulay's comment is from his diary, October 4, 1852. George Sand's eulogy, which appeared in a periodical in which *Uncle Tom's Cabin* was being serialized, is reprinted in Fields, pp. 151-57.

6. The relation between HBS and George Eliot is shown in their correspondence. It is referred to by Blanche Colton Williams, *George Eliot, a Biography* (New York, 1936), pp. 125, 251. The reference to Gladstone is based on a letter reprinted in Florine Thayer McCray, *The Life-Work of the Author of Uncle Tom's Cabin* (New York, 1889), referred to hereafter as "McCray," p. 286. Mrs. Browning, who apparently did not admire HBS as writer, found her a delightful person, with a "largeness and fearlessness of thought" which embraced even spiritualism. "Never did lioness roar more softly" (quoted by Dorothy Hewlett, *Elizabeth Barrett Browning, a Life*, New York, 1952, pp. 333, 360-61).

7. Charles Reade's mistake was his belief that the *Key To Uncle Tom's Cabin* (1853) described HBS's preparation for writing her novel; see Wayne Burns and Emerson Grant Sutcliffe, "Uncle Tom and Charles Reade," *American Literature*, XVII (1945-46), 334-47. The varied influences of HBS on Mark Twain are suggested by Jay B. Hubbell, *The South in American Literature 1607-1900* (Durham. N.C., 1954), p. 833; Kenneth S. Lynn, *Mark Twain and Southwestern Humor* (Boston, 1959), p. 240; and Albert E. Stone, Jr., *The Innocent Eye: Childhood in Mark Twain's Imagination*

(New Haven, Conn., 1961), pp. 5, 9-10. Although such claims are not convincing, there can be no doubt of Mark Twain's respect and admiration for HBS.

8. Ruth Suckow, " An Almost Lost American Classic," *College English*, XIV (1953), 315-25; Lillian Beatty, "The Natural Man Versus the Puritan," *Personalist*, XL (1959), 22-30; James Baldwin, "Everybody's Protest Novel," *Partisan Review*, VI (1949), 578-85 (a double-barrelled attack on *Uncle Tom's Cabin* and the persistent defects of American social protest); Joseph Chamberlain Furnas, *Goodbye to Uncle Tom* (New York, 1956), a blistering attack on racism; Edmund Wilson, in the *New Yorker*, November 27, 1948, an enthusiastic article-review on the occasion of a new edition of *Uncle Tom's Cabin;* Leslie A. Fiedler, *Love and Death in the American Novel* (New York, 1960) and *No! in Thunder: Essays on Myth and Literature* (Boston, 1960).

9. References to Mrs. Stowe's magazine articles and sketches as "hack work" or to her lesser books as "pot-boilers" are unjust to the earnestness with which she strove, invariably, to do good.

Chapter One

1. Fields, p. 11. Since the incidents referred to in this chapter are described in all the biographies, usually at length, notes to indicate specific pages are dispensable.

2. Charles Beecher, ed., *Autobiography, Correspondence, etc., of Lyman Beecher, D.D.* (New York, 1864), I, 149, 525; II, 11; Mae Elizabeth Harveson, *Catharine Esther Beecher, Pioneer Educator* (Philadelphia, 1932), p. 23.

3. This is the impression given by the autobiographical story, *Poganuc People* (New York, 1878), especially pp. 17-21, 128. It is one of Constance Rourke's chief contentions in *Trumpets of Jubilee* (New York, 1927). The strongest indictment of Lyman Beecher's educational policies is by Barbara M. Cross in her preface to the 1961 edition of his *Autobiography* (pp. xiii-xxxiii): among his children, all of whom found his God "intolerable," one went insane and committed suicide (James); another killed himself, probably intentionally (George); others had nervous breakdowns (Catherine, Harriet) or pathological headaches (Henry Ward) (p. xiii). Young Harriet's repression and rebellion are easy to exaggerate, and in later years she insisted that her childhood had been happy. "As a child we were wholesomely neglected" (*A Library of Famous Fiction*, New York, 1873, p. viii). How wholesome she thought her girlhood was while she was living it is another matter. The

unusual harshness of her family can be seen by comparing her girlhood with that of Miss Sedgwick, her senior (Mary E. Dewey, ed., *Life and Letters of Catharine M. Sedgwick*, New York, 1871), or Miss Susan Warner, her junior (Anna B. Warner, *Life and Letters of Susan Warner*, New York, 1909). Sandford Fleming, *Children and Puritanism; the Place of Children in the Life and Thought of the New England Churches, 1620-1847* (New Haven, 1933), fully documents from church sources and without reference to HBS or other writers of fiction, the contrast between the earlier New England strict treatment of children and the more benevolent and understanding appeal to be made by HBS. He credits the change largely to Horace Bushnell's *Views of Christian Nurture* (1847), which is, though important, too narrow a base for explaining the large-scale reorientation going back, in other social groups, at least as far as Jean Jacques Rousseau.

4. Charles Edward Stowe, *Life of Harriet Beecher Stowe* (Boston, 1890), p. 28. This book is referred to hereafter by the author's full name or initials.

5. Theological questions are thoroughly discussed in Charles H. Foster, *The Rungless Ladder; Harriet Beecher Stowe and New England Puritanism* (Durham, N. C., 1954). In brief, Lyman Beecher's theology was precisely that from which William Ellery Channing appealed in "The Moral Argument against Calvinism." Harriet's later departure from her father's views led her, not to Unitarianism, but to Anglicanism, her dead mother's creed. There is no doubt of the sincerity of her conclusion (however hard it may have been to live by during great misfortunes), as expressed by the heroine of *The Minister's Wooing* (1859): "Christ has given me peace" (p. 393); "Christ has given me the victory over sorrow" (p. 385).

6. Lyman Beecher Stowe, *Saints, Sinners and Beechers* (Indianapolis, 1934), p. 163.

7. HBS wrote of Mary Scudder, heroine of *The Minister's Wooing* (1859): "The very intensity of the repression under which her faculties had developed seemed, as it were, to produce a surplus of hidden strength, which came out in exigencies" (474).

Chapter Two

1. "Love *versus* Law," *The Mayflower; or Sketches of Scenes and Characters among the Descendants of the Puritans* (New York, 1843), p. 54. The original title of the story, as published in *The Gift* for 1840, was "Deacon Enos."

2. *Ibid.*, pp. 87-88. The italics are HBS's. "*Faculty* is Yankee for *savoir faire*, and the opposite virtue to shiftlessness" (*Minister's Wooing*, 1859, p. 2). "Them that has it, has it" (p. 56).

3. *Dred* (1856), II, 42. Calvin Stowe had also been a college valedictorian.

4. Lydia Huntley Sigourney, *Sketch of Connecticut, Forty Years Since* (Hartford, Conn., 1824), p. 4.

5. Miss Harriet E. Beecher, *A New England Sketch* (Lowell, Mass., 1834), reverse of title page.

6. *Illinois Monthly Magazine*, I (1831), 19.

7. The financial failure of the *Western Monthly Magazine* was caused by a religious controversy with Lyman Beecher; see John T. Flanagan, *James Hall, Literary Pioneer of the Ohio Valley* (Minneapolis, Minn., 1941), pp. 66-67. Although Hall transferred his major efforts from periodical journalism to banking, he did not revise his literary standards. In his brief "Autobiography," written in 1855, he takes pride in his purity of language, unpretentious style, moral delicacy, and American spirit. (*Ohio State Archaeological and Historical Quarterly*, Vol. 56 [1947], pp. 295-304). His racy *Legends of the West* (1832) are still noted for their local color and lively regional speech.

8. Charles Deering Mansfield, *Personal Memoirs* (Cincinnati, 1879), p. 295.

9. The four stories were reprinted from *Godey's*; see Lyle H. Wright, *American Fiction 1774-1850* (San Marino, Calif., 1939), pp. 124-25.

10. In *Godey's Lady's Book*, XVIII (1839), 115-22, and reprinted by Sarah Josepha Hale in *Woman's Record* (New York, 1852), a comprehensive annotated anthology, pp. 837-38.

11. Mrs. Hale's anthology shows the state of affairs; as does Rufus Wilmot Griswold's *The Female Poets of America* (1849; enlarged edition, New York, 1877). Frank Luther Mott's classic *History of American Magazines* (Cambridge, Mass., 1938) contains a wealth of material, particularly in volume two. Herbert Ross Brown, *The Sentimental Novel in America 1789-1860* (Durham, N.C., 1940), is substantial and well documented. A perceptive brief analysis is Ola Elizabeth Winslow, "Books for the Lady Reader, 1820-1860," in *Romanticism in America*, ed. by George Boas (Baltimore, 1940). On the whole the earlier references are the most revealing, since even such a lively book as Helen Waite Papashvily, *All the Happy Endings: A study of the Domestic Novel in America, the Women Who Wrote it, the Women Who Read it, in the Nineteenth Century* (New York, 1956), cannot do justice to the sentimentality of these writers.

12. Both *The Wide, Wide World* and *Stepping Heavenward* were available in cheap reprints a few years ago. Admiring biographies of both ladies were written by members of their families, and a revealing brief sketch of Mrs. Prentiss is by Marion Harland in *Our Famous Women* (Hartford, 1884), a sizable volume with contributions by Mrs. Stowe and others. Although *Stepping Heavenward* has been ignored by historians of the art of fiction (for good and sufficient reason), it is noted with a measure of justice by Willard Thorpe in his survey "The Religious Novel as Best Seller in America," in *Religion in American Life*, ed. by J. W. Smith and A. L. Jamison (Princeton, N. J., 1961), II, 211-12.

Chapter Three

1. Harriet Beecher Stowe, *Uncle Tom's Cabin, or, Life Among the Lowly* (Boston, 1878), p. 1. This edition has the advantages over the first edition (1852) of greater accessibility and an extensive author's introduction. Referred to hereafter as UTC. An impressive recent edition is published by Harvard University Press (Cambridge, Mass., 1962), with an authoritative introduction by the editor, Kenneth S. Lynn.

2. Harriet Beecher Stowe, *First Geography for Children* (Boston, 1855), p. 42: "God always makes those most prosperous who are most obedient to his laws in the Bible. The New England people own more ships, in proportion to their numbers, than any other country; and manufactures like those in the picture [on page forty of the geography] abound all over New England, especially in Massachusetts."

3. Charles Edward Stowe, p. 158; Forrest Wilson, *Crusader in Crinoline*, p. 277.

4. The phenomenal sales figures of UTC are estimated by James D. Hart, *The Popular Book; a History of America's Literary Taste* (New York, 1950), pp. 110-12, and by Frank Luther Mott, *Golden Multitudes; the Story of Best Sellers in the United States* (New York, 1957), pp. 117-21. According to Mrs. McCray (p. 121), the book was still selling in 1887 at the rate of 1,500 copies a month, and the New York *Times* book review section noted (March 18, 1962) that 21,342 copies of UTC had been sold during 1961 "in this country," divided among the eight editions then in print.

5. Henson's autobiography was first published in 1849 and later revised under the title *Truth is Stranger than Fiction* (Boston, 1858), with a preface by HBS. The phrases quoted or referred to occur on pp. 220-26 of an 1879 reprint.

6. Disputes about "identifications" are apparently endlessly fas-cinating to literal-minded antiquarians. Many "sources" have been given for the character of Eliza, as in the family biographies and by HBS in the final chapter of UTC, "Concluding Remarks," as well as in the preface to the 1878 edition; yet Eliza *in the book* is primarily the objectifying of Mrs. Stowe's own feelings as a mother. Though Topsy may have been based upon a specific servant known to HBS, she became less a human being *in the book* than a minstrel show stereotype or, as Leslie Fiedler has suggested, a picturesque blackness to balance the perfect whiteness of Eva. (*No! in Thunder,* Boston, 1960, p. 267).

7. Lyman Beecher, *Autobiography* (New York, 1864), II, 345.

8. Theodore Dwight Weld, *American Slavery as it is; Testimony of a Thousand Witnesses* (New York, 1839), published by the Amer-ican Anti-Slavery Society.

9. Quoted by Gilbert Hobbs Barnes, *The Antislavery Impulse 1830-1844* (New York, 1933), p. 231.

10. The quoted phrases are from issues of December 14, 1848, and July 22, 1847. The contributions referred to were published at various times between February 18, 1847, and April 22, 1852.

11. The importance of the Fugitive Slave Act to UTC has been recognized from the first. As late as 1905 a sturdy southerner, John C. Reed, of Georgia, charged that "the faithful guardians of American union had *Uncle Tom's Cabin* written on purpose to prevent the execution of the fugitive slave law." (*The Brothers' War,* Boston, 1905, p. 183).

12. Henry James, *A Small Boy and Others* (London, 1913), p. 263.

13. Now that "Uncle Tom" is widely used as a term of reproach for Negroes insufficiently assertive and self-respecting, Mrs. Stowe has been frequently accused of race prejudice. This is the charge against her made by Joseph C. Furnas in his *Goodbye to Uncle Tom* (New York, 1956), though he admits that her "puerilities" were "inadvertent," that she and her book were "merely blundering and overweening," and that she was not completely responsible for the "destructive racism" of George Aiken's play. Considering the period in which she wrote, Mrs. Stowe's tacit assumption of white superiority was no indication of intolerance. She believed, for ex-ample, in common, joint education of the races; she later regretted the emphasis on colonization in the concluding chapters of *Uncle Tom's Cabin;* and she advocated greater social and political equality than even Abraham Lincoln in the decade of the 1850's. (See Leon F. Litwock, *North of Slavery; the Negro in the Free States, 1790-1860* [Chicago, 1961], pp. 138-39, 255, 276-78.) Certainly George

Harris was no "Uncle Tom," and in our day Langston Hughes, who is emphatically no "Uncle Tom," has written a completely conciliatory introduction to the book, calling it "a moral battlecry" and "an appeal to the consciences of all free men." Many white readers have felt that Mrs. Stowe idealized rather than degraded her Negro characters, or that she "was wholly ignorant of the slave mentality." (For example, John Erskine in *Leading American Novelists*, New York, 1910; James F. Rhodes, *History of the United States* [New York, 1928 ed.], p. 322; F. Hopkinson Smith, *Literary Digest*, 45 (1912), 1225-26; William E. Woodward, *Years of Madness* [New York, 1951], p. 14.)

14. The heated debate which began then over the merits of UTC has never ceased. Not everybody liked it, or ever will. Objections came mainly, but not exclusively, from the South. Mrs. Chestnut, for one, did not deny that "Mrs. Stowe's exceptional cases may be true" (Mary Boykin Chestnut, *A Diary from Dixie* [Boston, 1949], p. 122); and the more than a dozen fictional "answers" fell flat (Herbert Ross Brown, *The Sentimental Novel in America*, pp. 259-64). In England, Gladstone was repelled by HBS's aggressive propaganda (John Morley, *Life of William Ewart Gladstone*, New York, 1921 ed., II, 72), and so was the American minister, James Buchanan, who referred to the book in several letters, without indicating that he had actually read it. (*Works of James Buchanan*, ed. by John Bassett Moore, New York, 1960, IX, 101, 108, 115.) Sensitive readers were distressed by the large element of cruelty, lust, and sadism, as painful in 1852 as similar exploitations of the seamy side of life by Erskine Caldwell and William Faulkner a century later. Such adverse criticism carried little weight against the general adulation which UTC received. As early as 1868 the New York *Nation*, in an editorial on "the Great American Novel" (VI, [January 9, 1868], 27-29) designated UTC as the nearest and only approach: "a picture of American life, national in scope, recognizable and valid." These are fighting words.

Chapter Four

1. The London *Times* review, September 3, 1852, was reprinted in New York as an eight-page pamphlet and also in the *National Anti-Slavery Standard*, September 30, 1852. The book would appeal, said the reviewer, to readers with strong hearts and weak intellects. Frank Luther Mott gives a graphic account of the excitement as reflected in the magazines (*A History of American Magazines*, II, 142-44); the quoted criticism is by no means en-

tirely favorable. The Stowes received many obnoxious letters, some of which, never seen by Mrs. Stowe, "badly spelled productions, evincing cowardly ruffianism, were taken with tongs by her husband and dropped, almost unread, into the fire" (p. 106). Much of the public abuse was reprinted in three antislavery papers: the *Era*, the *Liberator*, and the *Standard*. The single libel suit caused by the book was settled, after fantastic public charges and private negotiations, out of court (Forrest Wilson, *Crusader in Crinoline*, pp. 287-321).

2. William J. Grayson, "The Hireling and the Slave" (1854), as quoted by Vernon Louis Parrington, *Main Currents in American Thought* (New York, 1927-30), II, 107. See also Jay B. Hubbell, *The South in American Literature 1607-1900* (Durham, N. C., 1954), pp. 445-46.

3. New York: Pudney and Russell, printers, No. 79 John-Street, 1853.

4. The sins of the churches had been vigorously attacked by HBS's former fellow-Cincinnatian, the victim of the 1836 riots, James G. Birney, in *The American Churches, the Bulwark of American Slavery* (Newburyport, Mass., 1842). John Greenleaf Whittier, the only dedicated abolitionist agitator among the New England poets, repeatedly scourged the pro-slavery clergy as "hypocrites" and "blasphemers" (Lewis Leary, *John Greenleaf Whittier* [New York, 1961], pp. 44-45, 110-11).

5. James C. Derby, *Fifty Years among Authors, Books, and Publishers* (New York, 1884), pp. 520-21. The amanuensis was presumably either Eliza or Harriet, both of whom served as their mother's secretaries throughout the rest of her life.

6. Mrs. Stowe's pessimism regarding emancipation can be seen from a reference in *Dred* (II, 212), in her phrase *Utopian dream* (preface to 1878 *Uncle Tom's Cabin*, p. xxxi), and in the explicit statement of Mrs. McCray (p. 102): "Mrs. Stowe never expected to see the slaves free."

7. The dramatization of *Dred* failed to hold the stage, partly because of the organization of the novel itself, partly because of the adaptor's sentimental minstrel mannerisms. The "opening chorus" is typical: "Pretty Carolina Rose, won't you hear, won't you hear?" (John Brougham, *Dred: or the Dismal Swamp*, in *Modern Standard Drama*, Vol. XIX, no. 145).

8. Harriet Beecher Stowe, *Sunny Memories of Foreign Lands* (Boston, 1854); the characteristic phrases quoted in this paragraph appear in Vol. II, pp. 160, 332, and 228.

9. John Ruskin, *Letters of John Ruskin to Charles Eliot Norton* (Boston, 1904), I, 54. Macaulay was roused to fury by her mis-

representation of his conversation in *Sunny Memories*: "A mighty foolish, impertinent book. . . . What blunders she makes; . . . She cannot even see. . . . I am glad that I met her so seldom, and sorry that I met her at all." (G. Otto Trevelyan, *Life and Letters of Lord Macaulay* [New York, 1875], II, 302).

10. John Raymond Howard, *Remembrance of Things Past* (New York, 1925), p. 72. Mrs. McCray (p. 117) and Forrest Wilson (p. 400) note that she organized the preachers of New England in a mass petition to Congress against the Kansas-Nebraska bill, and Wilson adds that she became more than casually interested in national politics in 1856 (p. 417).

11. It was favorably received by the British public. According to Frank J. Klingberg "Harriet Beecher Stowe and Social Reform in England," in *American Historical Review*, XLIII (1938), 542-52, Mrs. Stowe's three visits to England were all highly successful. Another historian has speculated that her initial popularity there was due partly to the value of *Uncle Tom's Cabin* as anti-American propaganda. (Ephraim Douglas Adams, *Great Britain and the American Civil War* [London, 1925], I, 33.)

Chapter Five

1. Mrs. McCray (p. 416) describes *Woman in Sacred History* as "a superb volume which, in its plainest binding, sold for six dollars." It was issued in several forms, with poems and more chromos added, and sold in all about 50,000 copies (416-17). *Footsteps of the Master* lacked the lavish format, but it was reissued in *Religious Studies*, 1896, and as Vol. XV of the collected *Writings*. Both books were originally articles in the *Christian Union*. In the notes that follow, these titles are abbreviated as WSH and RS.

2. The entire composition was printed in Charles Edward Stowe's biography of his mother, pp. 15-21, and has been reprinted in later biographies.

3. The company failed because, according to John Raymond Howard, a member of the firm, it overstocked Beecher books when the Beecher-Tilton scandal knocked the bottom out of the market. (Howard, *Remembrance of Things Past* [New York, 1925], p. 306.)

4. The specimens selected can be found on pp. 49, 51, 63, 69, 80, 81, 149, 254, 328, 421.

5. Margaret Wyman has made the plausible suggestion that Mrs. Stowe's skepticism regarding woman suffrage, which is not observable in the December, 1870, installments of the serial, was her shocked reaction to the free-love agitation of Victoria Wood-

hull, which received unfavorable publicity in January, 1871. ("Harriet Beecher Stowe's Topical Novel on Woman Suffrage," *New England Quarterly*, XXV [1952], 383-91.) The contradiction, whatever its immediate cause, is not without parallel in Mrs. Stowe's other works.

6. *We and Our Neighbors*, pp. 48, 92, 95, 98, 147, 306, 342.

7. William Dean Howells, who reviewed the book (anonymously) in the *Atlantic Monthly* (Vol. 28 [September 1871], pp. 377-78) classified it as a sermon. "Mrs. Stowe could not make a dull or meaningless sermon," he averred gallantly, then added that it was one "which we should commend more for the good purpose characteristic of it all, than for its strength of exegesis or for the dramatic impersonation of its ideas."

8. *The Chimney-Corner*, p. 55.

9. *House and Home Papers*, p. 110. The italics are hers.

10. *The Chimney-Corner*, p. 22. The italics are hers.

11. A letter (number 5) in the Fields collection, Huntington Library, mentions her price for the *Atlantic* articles as $200 each. In her apprenticeship, before UTC, she had proudly claimed the ability to earn $400 a year from her writing (AF, 132).

Chapter Six

1. The history of the *First Geography for Children* (Boston: Phillips, Sampson, and Co., 1855) is obscure. Presumably it is a revision (or reissue) of the 1833 *Primary Geography for Children* (Cincinnati: Corey and Fairbank) by C. and H. Beecher. Although more than one hundred thousand copies of the earlier book are reported to have been sold, no copy has found its way into a public library where it can be examined. A comment in the 1855 book (p. 3) has encouraged the speculation that the revision was Catherine's work, although Harriet was named as author to stimulate sales (Forrest Wilson, p. 406); but Mrs. McCray stated (p. 224) that HBS "busied herself" writing it "in leisure hours."

2. HBS, *Oldtown Folks* (1869), p. 229. More eulogistic, but difficult to quote briefly, are the passages on Mather on pp. 285-86, 328-29.

3. Cotton Mather, *The Wonders of the Invisible World* (London, 1862, ed.), p. 12.

4. I regret my inability to agree fully with the more than competent scholars who have praised Sam Lawson's yarns—Walter Blair, for one, in his *Native American Humor* (1937). The stories had many virtues, but readability is not one which has survived.

5. *Poganuc People,* p. 308. For the greater religious power of women than preachers, see also *The Minister's Wooing,* p. 37, and "The Minister's Housekeeper" in *Oldtown Fireside Stories.*

6. Sarah Orne Jewett, *Letters of Sarah Orne Jewett,* edited by Annie Fields (Boston, 1911), p. 47.

7. *Pearl of Orr's Island,* pp. 396, 75, 45. Mrs. Stowe's son Henry had lately died.

8. P. 567. The italics are Mrs. Stowe's.

9. Mrs. McCray (p. 281) quotes Dr. Park's statement. Calvin Stowe also unsuccessfully urged changes in the theological references (Stowe and Stowe, p. 250). Charles H. Foster gives a clear account of the departures from biographical truth, with an explanation of the probable personal reasons for them (*The Rungless Ladder* [Durham, N. C., 1954], pp. 87-90).

10. This preference has not been unanimous. Mrs. McCray, for one, discussed *The Minister's Wooing* with unsurpassable enthusiasm. Later readers, with less enthusiasm (rejecting *Oldtown Folks* as a novel, because of its shapelessness or its discursiveness) prefer *The Minister's Wooing* as a more acceptable taste of Mrs. Stowe's New England. (See Alexander Cowie, *The Rise of the American Novel* [New York, 1948], pp. 463, 455.) Although the lengthy expositions of New England theology in *Oldtown Folks* have repelled some readers, they are probably Mrs. Stowe's greatest achievement as an interpreter of American life. Her insight into New England preachers, particularly the conservative types, is vouched for by many authorities, including Austin Warren (*New England Saints* [Ann Arbor, 1956], pp. 23-24, 32-33, 184). Her mature approach to the subject is shown as early as 1858: "It is a mark of a shallow mind to scorn these theological wrestlings and surgings; they have had in them something even sublime." (*Atlantic Monthly,* I [1858], 478).

11. *Agnes of Sorrento* (Boston, 1862), pp. 150-51, 112.

12. The passages quoted in this paragraph occur on pp. 34, 291, 186. The italics appear in the original.

13. The quoted phrases in this paragraph are taken from HBS's correspondence, Fields, pp. 304, 381.

14. Later accounts of the trial have been anti-Beecher. A particularly lively one, based on the court records and contemporary news stories, is by Robert Shaplin, *Free Love and Heavenly Sinners; the Story of the Great Henry Ward Beecher Scandal* (New York, 1954).

15. *Palmetto-Leaves* (Boston, 1873), pp. 113, 138.

16. Mrs. Stowe's life in Florida is best described in the local history by Mary B. Graff, *Mandarin on the St. Johns* (Gainesville, Fla., 1953), pp. 47-85, from which I have borrowed a number of

details. Much earlier, however, Sidney Lanier had remarked that Mandarin's principal celebrity was Mrs. Stowe's home.

Chapter Seven

1. An account of *Old and New* can be found in the *Life and Letters of Edward Hale*, by Edward E. Hale, Jr. (Boston, 1917), II, 97-119.

Chapter Eight

1. In 1886 she wrote, for her son's biography, that in her girl-hood "I was very much interested in poetry, and it was my dream to be a poet." (Charles Edward Stowe, p. 32; Fields, p. 43; Forrest Wilson, p. 69.) She continued working in verse and produced a number of respectable religious lyrics and hymns.

2. *A Library of Famous Fiction* (New York, 1873), p. viii.

3. On *Pilgrim's Progress*: "The loveliest and richest specimen of pure, tender, homely Saxon English which is to be found in any book *except* the Bible" (*ibid.*, ix; italics by HBS). References to Bunyan's book occur in most of her novels, including UTC, *The Minister's Wooing*, and *Oldtown Folks*. For unfamiliar passages praising Bunyan, see her articles in *Hearth and Home*, January 23, 1869, and the *Christian Union*, January 1, 1873.

4. This magazine article (*Atlantic Monthly*, XXIV [September, 1869], 295-313), "The true Story of Lady Byron's Life," one of the most discussed of the century, reduced the circulation of the *Atlantic* from 50,000 to 35,000. Nevertheless it was also hailed, as by the *Nation*, as "one of the greatest successes ever achieved in any country" (Mott, *History of American Magazines*, II, 505). Mrs. Stowe received much unfavorable criticism, and even trashy sensational magazines had a chance to express their shock, real or imagined, at finding such a scandalous article in the staid *Atlantic*. (Mary Noel, *Villains Galore; the Hey-day of the Popular Story Weekly*, [New York, 1954], pp. 302-03.)

5. A summary of this controversy, with an extensive bibliography, is in Samuel C. Chew, *Byron in England* (New York, 1924), pp. 278-83. Ethel Colburn Mayne, *Byron* (New York, 1924, 2nd edition) describes Mrs. Stowe's book as a mixture of "invective and sanctification," a combination of carelessness, contradiction, and self-deception; "never had truth so poor an advocate" (pp. 237, 446).

6. Richard Croom Beatty, *Bayard Taylor: Laureate of the Gilded Age* (Norman, Okla., 1936), p. 266.

7. The best account of *Cleon*, with the most quotation, is in Fields, pp. 43-49.

8. John T. Morse, Jr., *Life and Letters of Oliver Wendell Holmes* (Boston, 1896), II, 179. The italics are Holmes's.

9. Henry Adams, *Letters of Henry Adams* (Boston, 1930), p. 168.

10. These feats are noted in the biographies. On her verbal memory of Scott's verse see Lyman Beecher Stowe, *Saints, Sinners and Beechers*, p. 229; on the repetitive reading of *Ivanhoe*, HBS, "Answer to Correspondence," *Hearth and Home*, February 13, 1869.

11. In *Queer Little People* (Boston, 1867), p. 173. See also "Literary Epidemics," *Evangelist*, July 28, 1842, and *Poganuc People* (1878), pp. 131-32.

12. The details in this paragraph are assembled mainly from *Sunny Memories*, I, 195-220. In other places HBS misquotes familiar lines and makes a common error in giving the name of Shakespeare's son (II, 104; I, 150, 211). She was convinced that Shakespeare's mother was the original model for Desdemona (I, 203).

13. These casual references follow the course of European literature from Homer, Aeschylus, and Plato, through Virgil (quoted in Latin), Dante, and Tasso, to Bossuet's sermons, Fénelon, Rousseau and Voltaire (twin menaces), and Chateaubriand. They also outline selectively, English literary history from Donne ("one might almost say her body thought"), Locke, Defoe, Addison, Pope, Dr. Johnson (his prayers), Gray, Goldsmith, Hannah More, Jane Porter, Coleridge, Thomas Moore, Carlyle and Tennyson.

14. Also: "In the strictest New England times *Sir Charles Grandison* was often recommended by clergymen, and lay on the toilet-table of godly young women" (*Library of Famous Fiction*, p. vii).

15. Fields, p. 169. Although HBS read more than an afternoon's "great deal" of Goethe's *Faust*, she did not hesitate to tackle a complete synopsis in two paragraphs for *Woman in Sacred History* (p. 304). A more personal reference to the "great poem" in *Footsteps of the Master* (RS, pp. 93-94) is a tribute to the purified Margaret who "like a tender mother" saves the soul of the dying Faust in his "infantine weakness." HBS approved of the "wonderful mind" which recognized that even a fallen woman embodies "the eternal womanly [which] draws us upward and onward."

16. Fields, pp. 317, 342. See also articles by HBS in *Hearth and Home*, January 16 and 23, 1869. Even so, she wrote Mrs. Fields, "Hawthorne ought to have lived in an orange grove in Florida" (AF, p. 343).

17. Mrs. Stowe had been brought up to regard another great Victorian novelist, Charles Dickens, with suspicion. See especially "Literary Epidemics—No. 2," in the *Evangelist*, July 13, 1843, where

she wittily attacks him as a poor moral influence. Among novels of social reform, she preferred Charles Kingsley's *Alton Locke* (1850) to anything she had read by Dickens (Forrest Wilson, p. 427).

18. Lowell was not completely frank with Mrs. Stowe. After the Byron article he wrote, but not to her, that her good intentions had not produced a good result, and that her evidence was unconvincing. (Lowell, *New Letters*, ed. by M. A. DeWolfe Howe, [New York, 1932], p. 146.)

19. Samuel T. Picard, *Life and Letters of John Greenleaf Whittier* (Boston, 1895), II, 419.

20. Charles Eliot Norton, *Letters of Charles Eliot Norton* (Boston, 1913), I, 186. This practice was not followed. Norton's own attitude toward Mrs. Stowe was entirely friendly (I, 164).

21. Thomas Wentworth Higginson, *Cheerful Yesterdays* (Boston, 1898), pp. 176-80. H. W. Longfellow also refers to this dinner, but without Higginson's wit (Samuel Longfellow, *Life of Henry Wadsworth Longfellow* [Boston, 1899], II, 387). Mrs. Stowe's skirmishes with alcohol amused even her friends. Mrs. Thomas Bailey Aldrich tells of accidentally getting her dead drunk (*Crowding Memories* [Boston, 1919], pp. 120-26). See also James C. Derby, *Fifty Years among Authors, Books, and Publishers* (New York, 1884), p. 521. Forrest Wilson indicates that on occasion she drank wine, even champagne (pp. 416-17).

22. On Bret Harte, Wilson, p. 557; on Cable, Arlin Turner, *George W. Cable, a Biography* (Durham, N.C., 1956), p. 112.

23. Girand Chester, *Embattled Maiden; the Life of Anna Dickinson* (New York, 1951), p. 106; *Nation*, VII (1868), 346-47.

24. McCray's biography of HBS, an advertisement following p. 440 of the text.

25. James T. Fields, *Yesterdays with Authors* (Boston, 1871), p. 15.

26. Elizabeth Cady Stanton, *Eighty Years and More* (New York, 1898), p. 264.

27. Annie Fields, pp. 315, 313. In a similar vein, letter number 7 in the Fields collection, Huntington Library, mentions a "critical revision" of her poems.

28. By today's standards she need not have been ashamed—whenever she wrote carefully. Several letters in the Fields collection of the Huntington Library (number 10, 18, etc.) concern suitable copyreaders to correct her style.

29. Howells, *Literary Friends and Acquaintance* (New York, 1901), pp. 138-39.

30. HBS was not greedy but, being both generous and improvident, she was usually short of money. Mrs. McCray who, as a poorly

paid professional writer, appears to have been unusually inquisitive about sales and prices, reported that *Sunny Memories* sold nearly 40,000 copies in Great Britain, and that American sales were unknown (p. 223); that *Men of Our Times* sold nearly 40,000 copies (p. 360) and that *Woman in Sacred History* sold "something like" 50,000 copies (p. 417). HBS made over $20,000 on immediate profits from *Dred* and, as she told Fields, $11,500 on *The Minister's Wooing* as a book (Forrest Wilson, p. 531). The *Atlantic* paid $200 an installment for *Agnes of Sorrento,* and *Hearth and Home,* which never paid her, owed $5000 for her year's contributions (Wilson, pp. 464, 544). James Hart (*The Popular Book,* p. 112) states that "after 1853 any book [novel?] with her signature had a sure sale of at least 150,000 copies." One of her mass-production serials brought $8000 for the newspaper rights (AF, p. 315).

Chapter Nine

1. Mark Twain, *Autobiography* (New York, 1924), II, 243.

2. Daniel Dulany Addison, *Lucy Larcom; Life, Letters, and Diary* (Boston, 1894), p. 146. Elizabeth Stuart Phelps tells similar stories in *Chapters from a Life* (Boston, 1896), pp. 134-37.

3. *Literary Friends and Acquaintance,* p. 140.

4. Charles Edward Stowe, inserted pages following title page.

5. Typical of the comparative critical appeal of Hawthorne, Poe, and HBS are the lists of the year's scholarly productions in the latest (1961) PMLA bibliography (Vol. LXXVII, no. 2B): Hawthorne, items 4949-4988; Poe, items 5059-5093; HBS, items 5099-5100. The difficulty in interpreting Poe is made obvious in such a recent study as that by Vincent Buranelli, *Edgar Allan Poe* (New York, 1962), "Secondary Studies," pp. 145-51. Popular interest in HBS as a person is still great enough to produce such a biography as Johanna Johnston's *Runaway to Heaven: The Story of Harriet Beecher Stowe* (Garden City, N. Y., 1963)

Selected Bibliography

PRIMARY SOURCES

Lists of Mrs. Stowe's books are printed in Merle Johnson, *American First Editions* (New York, 1936) and in *Literary History of the United States*, Vol. III (New York, 1948). The most detailed bibliographical description of her books, to 1860, including British editions, translations, and adaptations, is in Joseph Sabin, *Bibliotheca Americana* (New York, 1933-34), XXIV, 33-37 (items 92395-92624). The following titles are those referred to in the present study.

Books

Agnes of Sorrento. Boston: Ticknor and Fields, 1862.

The Chimney-Corner, by Christopher Crowfield, *pseud*. Boston: Ticknor and Fields 1868.

Dred: A Tale of the Great Dismal Swamp. Boston: Phillips Sampson and Co., 1856. 2 vols.

First Geography for Children. Boston: Phillips, Sampson, and Co., 1855.

Footsteps of the Master. New York: J. B. Ford and Co., 1877.

House and Home Papers, by Christopher Crowfield, *pseud*. Boston: Ticknor and Fields, 1865.

A Key to Uncle Tom's Cabin. Boston: John P. Jewett and Co., 1853.

Lady Byron Vindicated. Boston: Fields, Osgood, and Co., 1870.

A Library of Famous Fiction. New York: J. B. Ford and Co., 1873.

Little Foxes, by Christopher Crowfield, *pseud*. Boston: Ticknor and Fields, 1866.

Little Pussy Willow. Boston: Fields, Osgood, and Co., 1870.

The Mayflower: or, Sketches of Scenes and Characters among the Descendants of the Puritans. New York: Harper and Brothers, 1843.

The May Flower, and Miscellaneous Writings. Boston: Phillips, Sampson, and Co., 1855.

Men of Our Times; or, Leading Patriots of the Day. Hartford: Hartford Publishing Co., 1868.

The Minister's Wooing. New York: Derby and Jackson, 1859.

My Wife and I: or, Harry Henderson's History. New York: J. B Ford and Co., 1871.

Oldtown Folks. Boston: Fields, Osgood, and Co., 1869.

Palmetto-Leaves. Boston: J. R. Osgood and Co., 1873.

The Pearl of Orr's Island: A Story of the Coast of Maine. Boston: Ticknor and Fields, 1862.

Pink and White Tyranny, a Society Novel. Boston: Roberts Brothers, 1871.

Poganuc People, Their Loves and Lives. New York: Fords, Howard and Hulbert, 1878.

Queer Little People. Boston: Ticknor and Fields, 1867.

Religious Studies, Sketches and Poems. Boston: Houghton, Mifflin and Co., 1896.

Sam Lawson's Oldtown Fireside Stories. Boston: J. R. Osgood and Co., 1872.

Sunny Memories of Foreign Lands. Boston: Phillips, Sampson, and Co., 1854. 2 vols.

Uncle Tom's Cabin; or, Life among the Lowly. Boston: Houghton, Osgood and Co., 1878. (This is a new edition, with extensive introductory matter. The first edition, in two volumes, was published by John P. Jewett and Company, 1852.)

We and Our Neighbors: Records of an Unfashionable Street. New York: J. B. Ford and Co., 1875.

Woman in Sacred History. New York: J. B. Ford and Co., 1873.

The Writings of Harriet Beecher Stowe. Riverside edition. 16 vols. Boston: Houghton, Mifflin and Co., 1896.

Uncollected Writings by Mrs. Stowe

"Among the Berkshire Hills." *Hearth and Home,* Sept. 18, 1869.

"The Andover Portfolio: Maine, Awake." *National Era,* July 20, 1854.

"Answers to our Correspondence." *Hearth and Home,* Feb. 13, 1869.

"Anti-Slavery Literature." *Independent,* Feb. 21, 1856.

"An Appeal to the Women of the Free States." *Independent,* Feb. 23, 1854.

"At Sea." *Christian Union,* XIV (1876), 510.

"Atonement—a Historical Reverie." *Evangelist,* Dec. 28, 1848.

"Aunt Katy." *Christian Union,* June 25, 1870.

"Bird Flights Southward." *Christian Union,* Jan. 21, 1874.

"A Bird's-Eye View of the West." *Christian Union,* Nov. 12, 1873.

"Books." *Independent,* Nov. 1, 1855.

"A Brilliant Success." *Independent,* Sept. 30, 1858.

"Bring up your Child in the Way he should go." Cincinnati *Journal,* June 2, 1836.

"Business Men's Prayer Meetings." *Independent,* April 8, 1858.

"Can I Write?" *Hearth and Home,* Jan. 9, 1869.

Selected Bibliography

"The Captain's Story." *Our Continent*, II (1882), 789-93.
"A Card." *Independent*, Nov. 21, 1861.
"The Cheapness of Beauty." *Hearth and Home*, March 20, 1869.
"Christmas Day North and South." *Christian Union*, Dec. 18, 1872.
"The Church and the Slave Trade." *Independent*, Nov. 1, 1860.
"The Colored Labor of the South." *Hearth and Home*, July 3, 1869.
Correspondence of the Parker-Stowe libel suit. *National Era*, Oct. 21, 28, 1852; also in part in the *Independent*, Oct. 7, 1852.
"Country and City." *Hearth and Home*, July 17, 1869.
"A Country Sunday." *Hearth and Home*, Sept. 25, 1869.
"Croquet, Butterflies, Birds, Sunshine and Moonlight in Florida." *Christian Union*, XIII (1876), 244.
"The Dancing School." *Evangelist*, April 6, 13, 1843.
"Deacon Enos." *The Gift* for 1840, pp. 144-87. Reprinted under title "Love *versus* Law."
"The Deacon's Dilemma." *Independent*, Nov. 22, 1860.
"The Death of Another Veteran." *Christian Union*, Jan. 7, 1874.
"De Rance and Fenelon—a Contrast." *Evangelist*, July 7, 1842.
"Does God Answer Prayer?" *Christian Union*, Nov. 13, 1872.
"Don't You Like Flowers?" *National Era*, Aug. 24, 1854.
"The Drunkard Reclaimed." *Evangelist*, Nov. 30, Dec. 7, 1839.
"The Duty of Being Happy." *Christian Union*, XII (1875), 130-31.
"The Education of Freedmen." *North American Review*, 128 (1879), 605-15.
"Eliza. From My Aunt Mary's Bureau." *Godey's Lady's Book*, XX (1840), 24-26.
European Letters, 1859-1860. *Independent*, Dec. 1, 1859, to Aug. 23, 1860. Twenty-three in all, printed in issues of Dec. 1, 8, 15, 22, 29, 1859, and Jan. 5, 12, 19, Feb. 16, April 5, 12, 19, 26, May 3, 10, June 21, 28, July 5, 12, 19, 26, August 23, 1860.
"Faces on the wall." *Christian Union*, Dec. 6, 1871.
"A False Position." *Independent*, Oct. 7, 1858.
"Faults of Inexperienced Writers." *Hearth and Home*, Jan. 23, 1869.
"The Fisherman Caught," verse translated from Goethe. *Lady's Book*, XXIII (1841), 11.
"Florida Again." *Hearth and Home*, May 15, 1869.
"The Florida Hegira." *Christian Union*, Dec. 2, 1874.
"Four Scenes in the Life of a Country Boy." *Hearth and Home*, July 24, 31, Aug. 7, 14, 1869.
"The Freeman's Dream: A Parable." *National Era*, Aug. 1, 1850.
"From the St. John's, South, to the St. John's, North." *Hearth and Home*, July 5, 1869.
"Fruits of the Revival." *Independent*, July 8, 1858.

"Getting Ready for a Gale." *Independent,* April 25, 1861.
"Getting Used to it." *Independent,* Dec. 13, 1860.
"Greeting." *Hearth and Home,* Dec. 26, 1868.
"Growing Things." *Hearth and Home,* March 6, 1869.
"The Handy Man." *Hearth and Home,* Aug. 21, 1869.
"The Happy Valley." *Christian Union,* Aug. 7, 1872.
"Hartford." *Hearth and Home,* Oct. 30, 1869.
"Hedged In." *Christian Union,* April 30, 1870.
"Heinrich Stilling." *Evangelist,* Feb. 6, 1851.
"A Heroic Squash." *Christian Union,* XII (1875), 229-30.
"The Higher Christian Life." *Independent,* March 17, May 19, 1859.
"Home Gardens." *Independent,* Feb. 11, 1858.
"Homeward from Canada." *Hearth and Home,* June 12, 1869.
"Horace Greeley." *Christian Union,* Dec. 11, 1872.
"Hot Weather Observations." *Christian Union,* Sept. 11, 1872.
"Hot Weather Religion." *Christian Union,* XIV (1876), 33.
"The Hour and the Man." *Independent,* Sept. 12, 1861.
"How may I know that I can make a writer?" *Hearth and Home,* Jan. 30, 1869.
"How shall I learn to write?" *Hearth and Home,* Jan. 16, 1869.
"How to Treat Babies." *Hearth and Home,* Feb. 6, 1869.
"I believe in the Resurrection of the Body." *Christian Union,* Oct. 30. 1872.
"Immediate Emancipation." *Evangelist,* Jan. 2, 1845; reprinted under the title "Uncle Sam's Emancipation."
"Independence." *National Era,* Jan. 30, 1851.
"The Indians at St. Augustine." *Christian Union,* April 18, 25, 1877.
"The Interior or Hidden Life." *Evangelist,* April 17, June 19, 1845.
"Is there a good time coming?" *Christian Union,* XII (1875), 106-7.
"Is there Anything in it?" *Christian Union,* May 14, 1870.
"Isabelle and her Sister Kate, and their Cousin." *Western Monthly Magazine,* II (1834), 72-75.
"Jesus." *Evangelist,* Feb. 19, 1846.
"The Journey North." *Hearth and Home,* May 22, 1869.
"Jubilee Days." *Christian Union,* July 10, 1872.
"Lenten Meditation." *Christian Union,* XI (1875), 171-72.
"Letter from Andover." *Independent,* Jan. 25, 1855.
"Letter from Andover," denouncing the London *Times. Independent,* June 13, 1861.
"Letter from Andover," urging the English to aid liberty. *Independent,* June 20, 1861.
"Letter from a Verandah." *Christian Union,* XII (1875), 465-66.
"Letter from Boston." *Independent,* Jan. 4, 1855.
"Letter from Florida." *Christian Union,* Feb. 7, 1877.

Selected Bibliography

"Letter from Florida: Out of the Fire." *Christian Union*, XIII (1876), 211-12.

"A Letter from Mrs. Stowe," from Boston. *National Era*, Feb. 15, 1855.

"Letter from Mrs. Stowe," from the continent. *National Era*, Sept. 8, 1853.

Letter on Holmes. *Critic*, II, n. s. (Aug. 30, 1884), 106.

Letter to Daniel Reaves Goodloe, from Andover, 1853. *Publications of the Southern History Association*, II (1898), 124-27.

Letter to Dr. Joel Parker. *National Era*, June 24, 1852.

"Letter to Lord Shaftesbury." *Independent*, Aug. 1, 1861.

"Letters from Europe." *Independent*, Jan. 22, 29, Feb. 5, April 23, 1857.

"Life at the White Mountains." *Christian Union*, Sept. 4, 1872.

"Literary Epidemics—No. 1." *Evangelist*, July 28, 1842.

"Literary Epidemics—No. 2." *Evangelist*, July 13, 1843.

"A Look behind the Veil." *Christian Union*, Nov. 5, 1870.

"Lord, if thou hadst been there!" *Evangelist*, Sept. 11, 1845. Reprinted in England as a pamphlet, *Worldly Conformity, the Cause and the Cure*, and in *The May Flower* as "The Elder's Feast."

"Mark Meridan." *Godey's Lady's Book*, XXII (1841), 242-44.

"Meditations from our Garden Seat." *Independent*, Aug. 9, 1855.

"Old Testament Pictures—No. 1." *Evangelist*, Nov. 14, 1844.

"Olympiana." *Godey's Lady's Book*, XVIII 1839), 241-43.

"On the Ministrations of Departed Spirits in this World." *Evangelist*, Jan. 25, 1849. Reprinted in *The May Flower* as "The Ministrations of our Departed Friends."

"One More Ascended." *Christian Union*, XII (1875), 318-19.

"The Only Daughter." *Godey's Lady's Book* XVIII (1839), 115-22.

"Our Early Rose Potatoes." *Hearth and Home*, Oct. 16, 1869.

"Our Friends in Heaven." *Independent*, Jan. 3, 1856.

"Our Lord's Bible." *Christian Union*, July 13, 1870.

"A Parable." *Evangelist*, Feb. 24, 1842.

"Pins in Pussy's Toes." *Christian Union*, Aug. 14, 1872.

"The President's Message." *Independent*, Dec. 20, 1860.

"The Prince." *Independent*, Oct. 18, 1860.

"Reading for Girls, Again." *Hearth and Home*, June 26, 1869.

"The Recent Revival." *Independent*, July 15, 1858.

"Religious Crises." *Independent*, March 25, 1858.

"The Revival." *Independent*, March 11, 1858.

"Rights of Dumb Animals." *Hearth and Home*, Jan. 2, 1869.

"St. Michael and All Angels." *Christian Union*, Oct. 22, 1870.

"Saratoga." *Christian Union*, Aug. 14, 1872.

"Saturday Afternoon." *Hearth and Home*, Oct. 2, 1869.

"The Scientists and Prayer." *Christian Union,* Nov. 27, 1872.

"Sea-Shore and Mountain." *Hearth and Home,* Sept. 11, 1869.

"The Second Coming—A Vision." *Christian Union,* old series, III, no. 51, Dec. 25, 1869.

"The Secret of Peace." *Christian Union,* XIII (1876), 113.

"Shadows on the Hebrew Mountains." *Independent,* 1854. Ten articles: Jan. 5, 19, 26, Feb. 2, 23, March 6, Oct. 26, Nov. 23, Dec. 7.

"A Sign of our Times." *Christian Union,* XIII (1876), 92-93.

"Signs of the Times." *Christian Union,* July 9, 1870.

Six pleas for immediate emancipation, 1862. *Independent,* July 31, Aug. 7, 21, 28, Sept. 4, 11.

"The Snow Siege." *Independent,* Feb. 26, 1855.

"Southern Christmas and New Year." *Christian Union,* XIII (1876), 44.

"Spiritualism." Four articles. *Christian Union,* Sept. 3, 10, 24, Oct. 1, 1870.

"Spring Breathings." *Independent,* June 14, 1855.

"Spring in Amherst." *Christian Union,* XIII (1876), 447-48.

"Stephen, the first Martyr." *Christian Union,* XIV (1876), pp. 288-89.

"Story of a Grain of Mustard Seed." *Christian Union,* July 24, 1872.

"A Suggestion on a Difficult Subject." *Christian Union,* June 4, 1870.

"Sunday in the White Mountains." *Christian Union,* XII (1875), 209-11.

"The Talisman." *Christian Union,* XII (1875), pp. 63-64.

"Things that cannot be shaken." *Independent,* Nov. 12, 1875.

"Thoughts from my Garden Seat." *Independent,* Sept. 6, 1855.

"Touching Florida." *Christian Union,* XII (1875), 154.

"Transplanting—A Parable." *Christian Union,* Aug. 21, 1872.

"The Traveler's Talisman." *Christian Union,* Aug. 20, 1870.

"Travelling Manners." *Hearth and Home,* May 1, 1869.

"Uncle Enoch." *Evangelist,* May 30, 1835.

"Under the Orange Trees." *Hearth and Home,* April 10, 17, 24, 1869.

"The Unfaithful Steward." *Evangelist,* April 7, 1842.

"The Valley of Humiliation." *Independent,* Sept. 5, 1861.

"Waiting by the River." *Christian Union,* Jan. 1, 1873.

"Western Pictures." *Hearth and Home,* Feb. 20, 1869.

"What Hath God Wrought!" *Independent,* Nov. 15, 1860.

"What is and What is not the Point in the Woman Question." *Hearth and Home,* Aug. 28, 1869.

"What Shall the Girls Read?" *Hearth and Home,* June 19, 1869.

"What shall we Raise in Florida?" *Hearth and Home,* May 8, 1869.

Selected Bibliography

"What will the American People do?" *Evangelist*, Jan. 29, Feb. 5, 1846.
"White Mountain Days." *Christian Union*, Sept. 18, 1872.
"Who Earned that Money?" *Hearth and Home*, Oct. 9, 1869.
"Who Ought to Come to Florida?" *Christian Union*, May 7, 1870.
"Who shall roll away the stone?" *Independent*, Sept, 3, 1857.
"The Widow's Mite." *Christian Union*, Oct. 15, 1873.
"A Winter in Italy." Twelve articles in the New York *Ledger*, weekly from Aug. 12 to Oct. 28, 1865.
"A Work of Faith." *Christian Union*, XIII (1876), 541.
"Writing—Commercially." *Hearth and Home*, March 13, 1869.
"The Yankee Girl." *Token and Atlantic Souvenir* for 1842, pp. 63-81.

SECONDARY SOURCES

Biographies

FIELDS, ANNE. *Life and Letters of Harriet Beecher Stowe*. Boston: Houghton, Mifflin and Company, 1898. Deeply and inherently sympathetic. (Most of my quotations from Mrs. Stowe's letters are taken from this book. For appreciations of Mrs. Fields, see M. A. DeWolfe Howe's book *Memories of a Hostess* [Boston, 1922] and Henry James's article "Mr. and Mrs. James T. Fields," *Atlantic Monthly*, CXVI [1915], 21-31.)
GILBERTSON, CATHERINE. *Harriet Beecher Stowe*. New York: D. Appleton-Century Company, 1937. Nicely written.
McCRAY, FLORINE THAYER. *The Life-Work of the Author of Uncle Tom's Cabin*. New York: Funk and Wagnalls, 1889. This unauthorized biography is expanded to 440 pages by the inclusion of long, eulogistic summaries of some of Mrs. Stowe's books.
STOWE, CHARLES EDWARD. *Life of Harriet Beecher Stowe*. Boston: Houghton, Mifflin and Company, 1890. Authorized family biography; contains the first printing of indispensable letters and other documents.
STOWE, CHARLES EDWARD, and LYMAN BEECHER STOWE. *Harriet Beecher Stowe: The Story of her Life*. Boston: Houghton, Mifflin Company, 1911. Centennial biography, with new material from family archives.
WILSON, FORREST. *Crusader in Crinoline: The Life of Harriet Beecher Stowe*. Philadelphia: J. B. Lippincott Company, 1941. By far the most vivid and complete biography; excellent documentation.

The best informed or most brilliantly written biographical sketches of Mrs. Stowe are:

ANTHONY, KATHARINE. "Harriet Beecher Stowe," in *Dictionary of American Biography*, Vol XVIII. New York: Charles Scribner's Sons, 1936.
BRADFORD, GAMALIEL, *Portraits of American Women*. Boston: Houghton Mifflin Company, 1919.
ERSKINE, JOHN. *Leading American Novelists*. New York: Henry Holt and Company, 1910. Biographical and critical link between nineteenth-and twentieth-century evaluations.
ROURKE, CONSTANCE M. *Trumpets of Jubilee*. New York: Harcourt, Brace and Company, 1921. An intuitive, persuasive interpretation of Mrs. Stowe's character in its cultural setting.
STOWE, LYMAN BEECHER. *Saints, Sinners and Beechers*. Indianapolis: The Bobbs-Merrill Company, 1934. Includes new material from the family archives.

Studies

FOSTER, CHARLES H. *The Rungless Ladder: Harriet Beecher Stowe and New England Puritanism*. Durham, N. C.: Duke University Press, 1954. Skillful study of the religious and theological elements in Mrs. Stowe's novels.
JORGENSON, CHESTER E., ed. *Uncle Tom's Cabin as Book and Legend*. Detroit: Friends of the Detroit Public Library, 1952. Guide to a centennial exhibition; contains brief informative articles, summaries of contemporary reviews, and a bibliography of scholarship.
STEARNS, E. J. *Notes on Uncle Tom's Cabin*. Philadelphia: Lippincott, Grambo and Company, 1853. The most urbane contemporary "rebuttal."

The best short surveys of Mrs. Stowe's novels are:

COWIE, ALEXANDER. *The Rise of the American Novel*. New York: American Book Company, 1948. With a valuable bibliography.
HUBBELL, JAY B. *The South in American Literature, 1607-1900*. Durham, N. C.: Duke University Press, 1954.
PARRINGTON, VERNON L. *Main Currents of American Thought*, Vol. II. (*The Romantic Revolution in America*) New York: Harcourt, Brace and Company, 1927.

Selected Bibliography

QUINN, ARTHUR HOBSON. *American Fiction, an Historical and Critical Survey.* New York: D. Appleton-Century Company, 1936.

VAN DOREN, CARL. *The American Novel 1789-1939.* New York: The Macmillan Company, 1940.

WAGENKNECHT, EDWARD. *Cavalcade of the American Novel.* New York: Henry Holt and Company, 1952. An unusually comprehensive survey, with a fine bibliography.

WHICHER, GEORGE F. [Harriet Beecher Stowe], in *Literary History of the United States,* pp. 581-86. New York: The Macmillan Company, 1948.

WILSON, EDMUND. *Patriotic Gore; Studies in the Literature of the American Civil War.* New York: Oxford University Press, 1962. A spirited and stimulating discussion, both biographical and critical, of Mrs. Stowe and her husband.

Useful studies of special topics have been mentioned in my notes, and others can be found in the bibliographies of Cowie, Jorgenson, and Wagenknecht, as listed above; in Lewis Leary, *Articles on American Literature, 1900-1950* (Durham, N. C.: Duke University Press, 1954); and in *Literary History of the United States* (Vol. III and supplement, 1948, 1959).

Index

Index

"Who Earned that Money?" 117
"Who Ought to Come to Florida?" 119
"Who shall roll away the stone?" 112
Woman in Sacred History, 79, 81, 82
"Writing—Commercially," 134
"Yankee Girl, The," 40, 41

Stowe, Henry, 73
Sumner, Charles, 76
Swift, Jonathan, 123-24

Taylor, Bayard, 125
Temperance Offering, The, 40
Tilton, Theodore, 106, 114, 119
Times, The (London), 62, 113
Token, The, 40, 41
Tolstoi, Leo, 9
Tourgée, Albion W., 122
Twain, Mark, 10, 138

"Uncle Tomism," 149-50 (Ch. III, n. 13)
Uncle Tom's Cabin (play by George Aiken), 7, 49, 149 (Ch. III, n. 13)

Violet, The, 40
Virgil, 130

Warner, Susan, 43-44
Watchman and Reflector, The, 77
Watts, Isaac, 129
Weld, Theodore, 56-57, 67
Wendell, Barrett, 141
Western Monthly Magazine, The, 32, 34-38, 43, 110
Whitney, Adeline Dutton Train, 133
Whittier, John Greenleaf, 10, 58, 59, 60, 126, 131, 132, 140
Wigglesworth, Michael, 95
Wilson, Henry, 76
Woodhull, Victoria, 85